OPPORTUNITIES

in

Travel Careers

WITHDRAWN

OPPORTUNITIES

in

Travel Careers

REVISED EDITION

ROBERT MILNE AND MARGUERITE BACKHAUSEN

VGM Career Books

Chicago   New York   San Francisco   Lisbon   London   Madrid   Mexico City
Milan   New Delhi   San Juan   Seoul   Singapore   Sydney   Toronto

The McGraw-Hill Companies

Library of Congress Cataloging-in-Publication Data

Milne, Robert Scott.
    Opportunities in travel careers / Robert Milne and Marguerite Backhausen.
—Rev. ed.
      p. cm.—(VGM opportunities series)
      Includes bibliographical references.
      ISBN 0-07-140589-5
      1. Tourism—Vocational guidance. I. Backhausen, Marguerite.
II. Title. III. Series.

G155.5 .M55 2003
917.3'0023—dc21   2002032963

2 3 4 5 6 7 8 9 0 LBM/LBM 2 1 0 9 8 7 6 5 4 3

ISBN 0-07-140589-5

Interior design by Rattray Design

McGraw-Hill books are available at special quantity discounts to use as premiums and
sales promotions, or for use in corporate training programs. For more information,
please write to the Director of Special Sales, Professional Publishing, McGraw-Hill, Two
Penn Plaza, New York, NY 10121-2298. Or contact your local bookstore.

This book is printed on acid-free paper.

And now I see with eye serene,
The very pulse of the machine;
A being breathing thoughtful breath,
A traveler betwixt life and death;
The reason firm, the temperate will,
Endurance, foresight, strength, and skill;
A perfect woman, nobly planned,
To warn, to comfort, and command;
And yet a spirit still, and bright
With something of angelic light.

—WILLIAM WORDSWORTH

For Gaby, the pulse of my machine.

—ROBERT MILNE

To Mom, whose support is immeasurable.

—MARGUERITE BACKHAUSEN

Contents

Foreword

PROFOUND FUNDAMENTAL structural changes in the U.S. economy—which have gone largely unnoticed—have escalated the importance of the travel and tourism industry to the nation's wellbeing. The travel industry's meteoric rise to become the nation's second-largest employer, with 7.8 million workers, ensures that its future as a major U.S. employer will be equally impressive.

The appeal of the travel and tourism industry as an employer is due not only to the quantity of jobs it provides, but to the diversity and quality of the jobs as well. The $545-billion travel industry provides a myriad of opportunities within such segments as airlines, rental car companies, attractions and amusement parks, travel agencies, hotel companies, national parks, tour operators, cruise lines, restaurants, railways, and campgrounds. Even within these segments, a variety of jobs exist whether one chooses to start as a frontline worker, in management, or on the corporate side of the organization.

The industry's rapidly rising need for talented employees has contributed to the overall quality of the jobs the industry has to offer. Travel- and tourism-related jobs defy traditional stereotypes about service industry jobs. They pay well and provide excellent opportunities for advancement, training, and even ownership; and they are rapidly growing in number. In fact, employment directly generated by travel grew 27.7 percent during the 1990s—far outperforming total (nonagricultural) U.S. employment growth of 19.6 percent—and promises to grow more than 21 percent in major travel industry sectors by 2006. This compares very favorably to other U.S. industries such as construction, which is projected to grow by 9.3 percent, and manufacturing, which is forecast to decline by 1.9 percent.

Today's travel industry has something for everyone. Consumers' interest in, enjoyment of, and need for our product continues to grow, which bodes well for the industry's future. Also, rapid changes in technology and communications are fueling major changes in how the travel industry does business. These advances are tearing down barriers and opening doors to the world marketplace, creating even more growth opportunities. In turn, these growth opportunities are generating a greater need for a talented, educated, and multilingual workforce to move this exciting industry forward.

Come be a part of it.

William S. Norman
President and CEO
Travel Industry Association of America

PREFACE

THE TRAGIC EVENTS of September 11, 2001, in the United States made us all realize the importance of the tourism and travel industry not only to the U.S. economy, but to the world economy as well. The Travel Industry Association of America (TIA) estimated in late 2001 that nearly $43 billion in spending by domestic and international travelers would be lost in the United States for 2001. In addition, 435,500 jobs directly related to travel and tourism would be affected. Worldwide tourism suffered as well, and preliminary figures indicate worldwide tourism receipts were down by 2.6 percent.

However, the strong belief of travelers worldwide is that to travel represents a fundamental freedom; this spirit will never cease to exist. As TIA's president and CEO, William S. Norman, stated, "Travel is one of our most fundamental freedoms, and it is our industry's responsibility to protect and preserve that freedom."

By the summer of 2002, TIA's Travel Confidence Survey indicated 77 percent of past-year travelers planned to take at least one pleasure trip during the summer, as compared to 72 percent who had such plans the year before at the same time. The amount of disposable income spent on travel, mode of transportation, and destinations would change—less air travel and staying closer to home—but people would be traveling nonetheless. Economic conditions continue to influence travel decisions, more so than safety, security, or inconveniences.

People will continue to travel, and jobs in the travel industry will continue to be a necessity. It is changing economic conditions and new technologies that will shift the types of travel jobs needed for the decade ahead.

Jason King, president and CEO of Yours in Travel Group, says, "Since September 11, nine million people worldwide lost their positions in tourism. While all industries were badly hurt from this event and the aftermath, the tourism and travel industries were hit the hardest. The travel industry is, however, rebuilding, but new candidates seeking opportunities in our field must be highly prepared."

In this new edition of *Opportunities in Travel Careers*, the majority of U.S. employment statistics such as earnings and job outlook were gathered from the U.S. Department of Labor, Bureau of Labor Statistics, for the year 2000. These figures were compiled prior to the events of September 11. Although the economic impact, as mentioned above, is substantial, only over time will the long-term effect of this tragic event on employment statistics be recognized.

1

Overview of the Travel and Tourism Industry

THERE ORIGINALLY WAS some confusion in the common uses of the words *travel, transportation,* and *tourism.* This confusion was aggravated in the period of America's early affluence, when some tourists who had acquired riches before they acquired culture made themselves ridiculous by their uncouth manners, loud voices, and conspicuous consumption, particularly when they were traveling in Europe. As a result, many tourists preferred to be called travelers, and tourist agencies became travel agencies, tourist bureaus became visitors' bureaus, and so forth.

Today, this artificial distinction has largely eroded away, and these words can now be used with their real meanings. A tourist no longer feels insulted to be called a tourist, and numerous governmental offices call themselves tourist promotion bureaus.

Further interesting definitions of these words are used at Niagara University's College of Hospitality and Tourism Management.

Transportation is defined as the movement of goods; *travel* is defined as the movement of people; and *tourism* concerns the entire business of leisure travel and related supporting activities.

This book concentrates on careers in all three of these broad fields, but selects those in which the work requires travel, direct service to travelers or vacationers, or promotion of travel and destinations. Thus, we shall discuss careers in the merchant marine because they entail travel, even though 97 percent of the workers on U.S. oceangoing ships are on tankers and freighters, and only 3 percent are on passenger ships. We shall omit consideration of workers in fields such as aircraft and automobile manufacture and auto repair. They serve the traveling public, but not directly, and little or no travel is required for their work.

Origin and Development of Travel

Travel has always been an important feature of people's lives. Historically, what we would call business travel began, in the most primitive sense, with staying alive—travel to obtain food. As civilization advanced, travel became a means to promote trade, consolidate governments, and provide communication.

Great migrations of peoples took place after disasters such as lava flows or floods had devastated their lands. This was business travel of the purest sort—they had to find new lands that would support them. Nomads in semiarid lands seldom stayed long in one place because their grazing animals would soon consume all the vegetation. Many groups of people who herded animals, such as the Laplanders with their reindeer, moved twice every year between summer pastures and winter havens.

As people began to specialize in what they could grow or make or mine from the earth, trade developed. The first traveling salespeople were emissaries to find markets for goods and to arrange for caravans or ships to deliver these goods.

Military travel also developed early, as warlike tribes conquered peaceful ones and moved into their territories. As empires grew, soldiers traveled ceaselessly between the capital and the farthest borders to supervise and carry orders and to impose the ruler's will. Regular messenger systems became fast and reliable as early as ancient times in Egypt, developing over the millennia into stagecoach and packet boat networks, the Pony Express, and modern courier and postal systems.

Thus, the stream of travelers has grown constantly—sailors, oxcart drivers, messengers, salespeople, armies, covered-wagon trains, herdskeepers—all intent on carrying on their own work or someone else's.

Another kind of travel developed in medieval times—educational travel. A young person learning a craft was apprenticed to a master craftsperson near home for a period of years to learn the basics; then the apprentice spent a year traveling to the workshops of masters of the craft in other countries, working there for a time to gain more skill and knowledge. Upon returning from these travels, the apprentice became a journeyman—one who had traveled and learned. Similarly, the typical university student would spend a "wander-year" visiting universities in other countries, studying under the most illustrious professors to be found, and polishing skills in one or two foreign languages. Travel thus achieved a new dimension, being performed not only for essential purposes, but to improve skill and knowledge.

Other nonbusiness travel was done for health reasons. Ancient Romans traveled to spas in Italy, Austria, and France seeking remedies for their ailments in curative water or mud. Only the wealthy could do this, of course, but physicians for hundreds of years have been prescribing travel as one way of improving health. They found that a change of air, of climate, of associations made people feel stronger. Europe's spas, which fell out of favor with American doctors as medical practice grew more scientific in the twentieth century, are not only still in business, but are attracting more people than ever before, including the patients of American doctors.

Travel for the pure pleasure of it—tourism—has been one of the special privileges of the rich since ancient times. Europe's spas, in addition to being health centers, were also social centers, with balls, picnics, plays, and concerts. They became more and more popular after stagecoaches were replaced by comfortable trains and sailing vessels by reliable steamships.

In America, too, there was summer travel by the rich to spas in Virginia, Pennsylvania, and Arkansas, as well as to summer estates at the seashore or in the mountains. The grand tour of Europe, which had become a tradition for aristocratic British students upon their graduation from Oxford or Cambridge, became a fashionable once-in-a-lifetime excursion of six months to a year for America's new industrial, mining, and railroad millionaires.

Wars have also stimulated travel. The Crusades, for example, gave Europe an interest in the Middle East that lasted for centuries, with trade and business travel flourishing between military campaigns. It was World War I that really brought intercontinental travel down to prices that middle-class Americans could afford, travel having piqued the interest of the millions of Americans who went to Europe to fight. Steamships were in their heyday, and the war had built up their passenger-carrying capacities.

At the same time, wide-ranging domestic travel came within the reach of Americans with the proliferation of inexpensive automobiles and hard-surfaced roads. As the automobile enabled people to travel further afield, such expensive resorts as Lakewood and Cape May, New Jersey, to which the wealthy had traveled by train from nearby cities, suddenly lost trade. Florida and southern California became destinations for mass travel, and many people began to travel during the winter to good mountain slopes for skiing. As a result, there was a burgeoning of beach, mountain, and ski resorts.

Then came World War II. Many millions of young American men and women were sent to Britain and all over Europe, to Hawaii, Alaska, the Philippines, China, India, Australia and New Zealand, the islands of the Pacific, North Africa and the Middle East, and finally, to conquered Japan, Germany, and Italy. These young people were fascinated with what they saw and did in other lands, and, naturally, they wanted to go back.

During the war years, aviation had come into its own. After the war, aerial troop transports were converted to serve the new traveling public as passenger aircraft, giving Americans a new kind of opportunity—travel to Europe for a vacation of only two weeks. U.S. aircraft factories converted to the manufacture of passenger planes and soon were supplying them to the new airlines that were springing up all over the world.

Travel now was possible for just about any Americans who wanted it—in their own cars throughout most of North America or on low-priced excursion and charter flights to other continents. Worldwide tourism increased 1,000 percent from 1950 to 1970, a phenomenal advance. To support this increase, there had to be a commensurate increase in the infrastructure that sustains tourism and attracts tourists—hotels, gambling casinos, amusement parks, marinas, airports, highways, beach facilities, ski resorts, aircraft, buses, cars, restaurants, entertainment and sports facilities, rental cars and boats, and a host of less visible items such as electricity, gas, telephone, and water supply systems in resort areas.

War-torn Germany and Japan, starting from rock bottom in 1946, worked hard and rebuilt their economies into powerful positions within twenty years. Profits filtered down, and soon German and Japanese tourists were being seen all over the world, along with British, French, and Italian tourists.

Tourism

Tourism requires some affluence, along with the feeling that travel is a desirable and rewarding activity. There are still about three billion people in the world who have neither the incentive nor the means to travel because their lives are totally occupied with the struggle for survival. And in many countries, citizens may have the intellectual curiosity and perhaps even the means to travel, but it is forbidden, except on the business of the government or on government-sponsored projects. Citizens of the United States tend to take travel for granted, but we should bear in mind that to the world's economically depressed and politically suppressed majority, it is an unattainable luxury.

Travel is coming to be regarded as a necessity in North America. Inflation in Europe and America, severe dollar devaluation, and an oil shortage imposed by the Arab nations reduced the number of Americans traveling to Europe in 1974 by 10 to 15 percent from the level of just a few years before. But Americans did not stop traveling. During the severest part of the oil shortage, people went to resorts near home, and many of these recreational areas had record years. The oil shortage eased, but unemployment and inflation worsened during the winter of 1974–75; yet Florida and other southern areas were jammed with tourists.

Dr. Louis F. Twardzik, chairman of the Department of Park and Recreation Resources at Michigan State University, said: "The great number of tourists crowding Florida resorts this winter wasn't really an unnatural phenomenon in times of social stress. Instead, it is merely an expression of the high value people place on their recreation today. The economic picture is severe enough to trigger a higher demand for recreation by people at all economic levels."

In the oil shortage of 1979, the earlier pattern was repeated. Travel in personal autos was considerably reduced, but this brought bonanza tourist business to resorts close to the cities. For longer journeys, travelers again crowded into buses, ships, trains, and aircraft.

Two points are of importance to the person considering a career in travel. First, recreational travel—available only to the rich during most of the world's history—has come to be regarded as a necessity in the United States and Canada for people of the lower middle class as well as for those of the middle and upper classes. It is very broadly based. Second, if travel by certain modes or to certain destinations becomes too expensive or otherwise difficult, people will switch to other modes or destinations, but they will continue to travel for pleasure. This indicates stability for the industry as a whole, regardless of the ups and downs for particular segments.

From 1985 on, it was noticed that people were taking more vacations, albeit shorter ones. Analysts deduced that this resulted from several changes in American life. In many families both husband and wife were working, which made it somewhat more difficult to get away for the traditional two weeks. There were more childless families, which made it easier to take spontaneous long-weekend vacations. There was less total leisure time because many people were working at two jobs, so they had to squeeze in brief vacations as their jobs permitted. The total effect on the tourism business was good because it helped to even out the number of people on vacation at any one time, thus contributing more stability to the business and steadier work for its employees. From 1985 to 1987, weekend trips increased by 46 percent.

Growth in the Travel and Tourism Industry

Tourism continues to be a major industry of the United States and of many countries of the world. Preliminary 2001 figures by the Travel Industry Association of America (TIA) reported the following statistics:

- The value of the U.S. travel industry is $545 billion.
- Tourism is one of the United States' largest service exports: the $90 billion spent in the United States by international visitors and $82.3 billion spent outside the United States by domestic travelers creates $7.7 billion in American trade surplus.
- Tourism is one of the country's largest employers, with eighteen million Americans directly involved in travel or travel-related jobs.

- Tourism is the first-, second-, or third-largest employer in twenty-nine states.
- Domestic U.S. travel has increased 6 percent from 1994 to 2000.

The Canadian Tourism Commission (CTC) reported that in 2000 tourism, from both domestic and international sources, has become a significant contributor to the Canadian economy:

- Total tourism revenues equal $54.1 billion.
- Tourism, as a percentage of the GDP, is 2.4 percent.
- Total direct tourism employment is 546,400, and the growth rate relative to the total business section is 0.5 percentage points faster.

An important demographic trend in the United States that will affect the travel industry in coming decades is the aging of the U.S. population. In 2001 the first of the "baby boom" generation (seventy-eight million people) turned fifty-five years old. This "mature traveler," according to a study conducted in 2000 by the Travel Industry Association entitled "The Mature Traveler (55+)," accounts for nearly one-third of all domestic travel in the United States. Travelers fifty-five years and older took nearly 179 million trips in 1999, up 5 percent over 1994.

In addition, the U.S. population continues to grow rapidly; from 275 million today it is forecasted to reach 400 million by 2050. Close to 30 percent of the population is currently under the age of twenty, offering enormous potential for future travel trade. Other trends, such as an increase in double-income households, rising education levels, and an increasing priority in the mindset of many to take vacations to escape the burdens of everyday life, affect a positive growth in travel.

Beyond the fact that travel is a huge and strong industry that should afford a good degree of stability in travel-related work, it has great intangible attraction. People in travel jobs are helping other people to go somewhere special, where they will relax and enjoy themselves. In our sedentary society, there are many who travel to find a challenge for their bodies—skiing, surfing, scuba diving, or mountain climbing.

With equal zest, others travel to find the challenges to the mind that appear in contrasting one's own feelings and actions with those of people in another country. Most groups believe they are inherently superior to others. Travelers make the discovery that theirs is not the only way of life, that they can learn from other cultures, and that their habits and thoughts are not even acceptable to many people. They also find that they can contribute an occasional workable idea in a foreign setting.

The travel worker, whose hours are passed with travelers seeking physical and mental challenge, relaxation, and change, finds constant stimulation from working with travelers and helping them fulfill their desires. Helping others travel stimulates one's own urge to go places, and being in the industry gives one special advantages for personal travel.

Perks in the Travel Industry

A special inducement offered by careers in travel is the possibility of traveling oneself—at nominal cost or totally free, or, better still, being paid to travel. Constant travel with a salary can be enjoyed as a member of a flight crew or a ship's company. Paid seasonal travel is available to tour directors—usually men and women who have worked their way up in a travel agency. Long-haul bus drivers, hostesses, and railroad train crews also are paid for constant travel.

Employees of airlines, passenger shipping lines, passenger rail lines, and bus lines, whether they travel in their jobs or not, usually are given liberal free or reduced-rate personal travel for themselves and their immediate families, beginning soon after they start working.

Travel agency personnel are so important in bringing business to air, rail, ship, and bus companies that these carriers offer them trips at very low rates and may offer free trips to familiarize them with new routes or cruises. Operators of tourist resorts or attractions and national tourism offices of foreign countries also give free familiarization ("FAM") trips to travel agents and sometimes to their staffs. Very low hotel rates usually are available to travel agency personnel. Additionally, employees of hotel chains usually can stay at their company's hotels at a fraction of the regular rates.

The Broad Variety of Travel Jobs

Transportation, travel, and tourism provide work for about one person in seven in the United States. The variety of occupations within the field or those closely allied to it is almost without limit. For example, a doctor, a manicurist, a chef, and a horn player all become part of the travel business if they work on a ship or at a resort such as Disney World.

The travel world, therefore, is not a single profession or vocation, but dozens of professions and occupations. Because travel and tourism is a conglomeration of several service industries, there is no single figure representing the travel and tourism economic output in the U.S. System of National Accounts (the accounting system that reports the gross national product). Two studies were put together in 1997—one for 1992 and the other for 1997—by a newly formed program called "Travel and Tourism Satellite Account" (TTSA) under the U.S. Department of Commerce. Efforts are currently underway to fund the continuation of these important studies, which also indicate the broad variety of jobs related to travel and tourism, including the following:

Hotels and lodging places

Eating and drinking places

Railroads and related services

Local and suburban transit

Interurban highway passenger transportation

Taxicabs

Air transportation

Water transportation

Automotive rental

Arrangement of passenger transportation

Miscellaneous amusement and recreation services

Racing, including track operation

Marinas

Libraries, museums, and art galleries

Botanical and zoological gardens

Members sports and recreation clubs

Motion picture theaters

Dance studios

Schools and halls

Theatrical producers

Bands, orchestras, and entertainers

Professional sports clubs and promoters

Gasoline service stations

Retail

Education for travel-related work is thus of many different kinds, and there is no single way to prepare for all travel jobs.

As with all large business organizations, marketing is vital to all of the major airlines, cruise lines, bus lines, hotel chains, and travel agencies. At the New School for Social Research in New York, the first master's degree program in Tourism and Travel Administration stresses marketing. The students, midcareer people working in travel, flock to the marketing courses. Marketing includes selling, but goes beyond salesmanship to find out what consumers want, why they prefer one product or hotel or airline over another, and much more. The effects on sales of public relations, advertising, merchandising, pricing, economics, airline scheduling, government regulation, and many other factors must be considered by a marketing director. Talented marketing people are directly in line to become vice presidents and presidents of their firms.

In the pages that follow, for each travel industry discussed, you will find information on its main career opportunities, what educational preparation you will need, and the specific steps you should take to get started on your career.

The figures represented in this book come from a variety of sources: the 1997 TTSA report, the U.S. Department of Labor (Bureau of Labor Statistics), and a number of trade associations, state agencies, and independent studies.

2

AIRLINES

THE SCHEDULED AIRLINES of the United States form a gargantuan industry, transporting more than 622 million passengers and more than 22 million ton-miles of cargo every year. This is accomplished with the investment of more than $89 billion in aircraft and ground facilities and the dedicated service of more than 670,000 employees.

The events of September 11, 2001, presented the United States airline industry with unprecedented challenges. Losses to the airline industry have been estimated at more than $7.7 billion in 2001, even with federal government assistance. However, signs of recovery are expected, and the airline industry, used to temporarily weathering losses due to skyrocketing fuel costs, economic recessions, or other factors, will pick up since an expanding population alone is bound to necessitate increasing air traffic.

Airline work is exciting, and the industry is still growing. Pay is fairly high in airline jobs, on average 53 percent higher than the national average, and working conditions are usually good. The field tends to attract adventurous people, so you are likely to discover social rewards in working with other lively and interesting employees.

Flight Attendants

This position used to be referred to as *stewardess*, *hostess*, or *steward*. In the past, the employee who served food and drink and attended to passengers' wants on U.S. and Canadian airlines had to be female, unmarried, young, attractive, and (in the early days of aviation) short—because of the low ceilings in passenger craft. At first, airline companies also required that flight attendants be nurses. Today approximately 15 percent of flight attendants are male, and there is a minimum height requirement on many airlines due to the height of the overhead bins.

According to the Association of Flight Attendants, AFL-CIO, which represents over 50 percent of the flight attendants of twenty-six airlines, in mid-2002 there were approximately one hundred thousand flight attendants.

Job Responsibilities

A flight attendant's main responsibility is passenger safety—to inform passengers of safety procedures and regulations and to enforce them. A flight attendant's job starts before the flight takes off with a briefing by the pilot on topics such as flight emergency evacuation procedures, weather conditions, or special passenger needs. A thorough check of emergency equipment, food, and beverage supplies and proper cabin conditions follows before the greeting of passengers aboard the plane.

Flight attendants also check passenger lists before takeoff and take care of flight reports, caterers' invoices, and requests for supplies or for special attention to equipment. Before takeoff, the flight attendant checks that passengers are properly seated and luggage is stored, and announces safety procedures in case of an emergency, such as oxygen and flotation equipment and the location of escape doors. After the flight takes off, the flight attendant serves the meals and drinks; answers questions about the flight; and distributes blankets, reading material, pillows, and so forth, as requested. Special care is given to unaccompanied children, the elderly, and handicapped persons. Prior to landing, an inventory is taken of headsets, alcoholic beverages, and moneys collected; landing announcements are made; and cabin safety checks are ensured for a safe and smooth landing. After the flight, a flight attendant reports on minor medication given to passengers, lost and found articles, and any other subjects that may need to be reported or addressed.

A flight attendant's job is not all glamorous. When a passenger becomes drunk and disorderly or sick, or even goes crazy or dies, it is the flight attendants who must cope with the problems. When there's an emergency landing, flight attendants must deploy slides and evacuate passengers swiftly. And the flight attendant is usually the first person to deal with a hijacker. Flight attendants must soothe angry, frightened, or sick passengers; serve drinks and meals as rapidly as possible; and take care of any special needs of passengers or the flight-deck crew. They often must work under tension, and on long trips, they may finish serving dinner at midnight and start serving breakfast two hours later. Vacation travel frequently starts Friday evening or Saturday morning and ends Sunday evening, so flight attendants often find themselves working in the sky on weekends instead of having time off.

On the other hand, flight attendants have considerable variety in their work and the added bonus of free or very inexpensive travel. In addition, they generally receive all the fringe benefits available in comparable office jobs.

Requirements

How times have changed! As mentioned above, it was once required that a woman be unmarried to be a flight attendant. Today, on average, a flight attendant must be at least eighteen to twenty-one years of age, married or unmarried. Excellent health, a well-groomed appearance, weight in proportion to height, minimum height to reach overhead bins (which vary by airline/aircraft), and vision corrected to 20/30 or better are the physical requirements of most airlines. Most airlines also give flight crews regular physical examinations, to make sure they remain in good condition and are able to cope with emergencies. Many airlines stress the ability to operate mechanical equipment, aircraft doors and window exits, evaluation slides, life rafts, and fire extinguishers, and they list associated weights for each type of equipment in flight attendant job descriptions. There are some variations in most of these qualifications, so if you don't fit a certain airline's specifications, look for an airline that fits yours.

All airlines stress the importance of professionalism, good customer service, and appearance.

A sample job description from a major U.S. airline states: "A flight attendant is in continuous contact with the public. As a flight attendant, you must perform your duties in a courteous and professional manner. You are responsible for providing the highest level of customer service to both our internal and external customers. Your behavior, appearance, and professionalism define our standard of excellence. The culture of our airline is to present a consistent, reliable, professional, customer-driven image."

A sample job description from a Canadian airline states: "The ideal flight attendant candidate presents a well-groomed appearance that is enhanced by a pleasant and outgoing personality. A sincere desire to be of service to customers is essential. The candidate must be pleasant, patient, well-mannered and have had previous experience working with the public. Above all, the flight attendant's role is highly service-oriented and very vital to the airline's success."

Most airlines require flight attendants to be high school graduates, although some say that a high school diploma or G.E.D. is preferred but not required. In actuality, most airlines want people who have had two years of college, nursing training, or experience in dealing with the public.

In most cases, U.S. immigration policy prevents airlines from considering for employment anyone who is not a U.S. citizen or who is an alien with a permanent visa. Since most airlines have a policy of hiring their own nationals, it is difficult for an American or Canadian to get a job with a European airline, for example, unless he or she has some special required qualification, such as fluency in several languages. Excellent English is expected by all airlines, and if you hope to work on an international route, a fair background in one other language is essential.

Air Canada requires its flight attendants to be Canadian citizens or landed immigrants and be able to speak at least two languages: English, French, and/or one of Air Canada's route languages.

Education and Training

Various private schools offer specialized training for flight attendant jobs, but generally speaking, such programs are not likely to help get you a job. Every airline either operates its own training facilities or sends its new flight attendants to a school, sometimes operated by another airline with which it has a contract. Training by the airlines is usually four to six weeks. Candidates go through intensive training that covers areas such as government rules and regulations, airline customer service philosophy, in-flight service, aircraft familiarization, and emergency procedures. Tests are given frequently, and some airlines require that a student must maintain an average of 90 percent to continue in the training program.

Once applicants have successfully completed an intensive training program, they may be assigned to an in-flight service base and are placed on reserve status. Reserve status flight attendants on duty are called in for flight attendants who are sick, on vacation, or have been rerouted. When not on duty, reserves must be available on short notice. Usually a flight attendant is on reserve for one year, but in some cities it can take up to five to ten years to get off reserve and be able to "bid" monthly for regular assignments.

The home base at which a flight attendant lives most of the time is called the *domicile*. This is not a dormitory, but a city in which the employee has an apartment. Oftentimes flight attendants starting out share apartments. If a flight attendant wants to remain permanently in the same city, he or she can choose an airline with short routes—generally called feeder lines—where there's a good chance of getting home to the same bed every night. On the long routes, a flight attendant is likely to spend several nights each month in a hotel room at the far end of the route.

Earnings, Advancement, and Job Outlook

According to the Association of Flight Attendants, in 2002 the median starting pay was $15,174 a year. The Bureau of Labor Statistics states that the median annual earnings of flight attendants were $38,820 in 2000, with the middle 50 percent earning between $28,200 and $56,610. Pay scales vary by airlines, seniority, and routes. On international flights (where facility in a foreign language is always desired, and often required), pay ranges from 12 to 20 percent higher. To get current hourly wages based on one's number of years as a flight attendant, refer to the flight attendant union websites (see the Sources of Information section at the end of this chapter).

With most of the major airlines, there is base pay for the first sixty-seven flying hours; and for each further flight hour, up to a maximum of eighty-five hours, there is additional pay. Pay raises are small but regular enough to be counted on, and there are allowances for meals away from home, limousines to and from airports, and uniform maintenance.

Advancement from the position of flight attendant comes with seniority and merit. The top position in the cabin crew is flight service director. At some airlines there is a special position called *purser*, the person who handles all cash collected during the flight for drinks, earphones, and merchandise.

Nonflying positions to which flight attendants can be promoted include jobs as instructor, customer service director, and recruiting representative. Flight attendants may be used in photographs by the airline's public relations staff.

Delta, which has historically insisted upon promotion from within, offers one example of promotion possibilities: after three years of flying out of Miami and Atlanta, one stewardess became secretary to Delta's director of engineering. Soon she was promoted to be one of five Delta female sales representatives. Within half a year, she became coordinator of women's services for the airline, overseeing the production of travel information and services to women.

The U.S. Federal Aviation Administration (FAA) views flight attendants not only as people who minister to passengers' creature comforts, but also as guardians of passengers' safety. To ensure passenger protection in case of emergencies, the FAA requires that there be one flight attendant for every fifty seats on an airliner. As aircraft grow in size, the number of flight attendants increases.

In the United States, the Association of Flight Attendants, AFL-CIO, represents the airline attendants of a number of airlines. The Association of Flight Attendants, International Brotherhood of Teamsters (IBT), and the Transport Workers Union of America represent attendants of other airlines. Several airlines have company unions (such as the Association of Professional Flight Attendants for American Airlines or the Association of Flight Attendants—United Airlines). Most flight attendants are union members. In Canada many flight attendants are members of CUPE (Canadian Union of Public Employees) Airlines Division.

In the late 1970s, the unions argued, bargained, and held long strikes. They succeeded in gaining recognition of their professionalism, higher pay, more consideration for their health and maternity problems, and improved rest facilities.

After the Airline Deregulation Act took effect at the beginning of 1985, however, the airline business was suddenly much more competitive than before. With no regulation of rates or routes or schedules, airlines were free to engage in rate wars, start new routes, drop service on routes losing money, and cut costs to the bone. One way of cutting costs was to reduce salaries. Continental did this, after much labor strife, by reducing salaries for new hires.

As part of the cost-cutting drive, some airlines started charging a fee for accepting a job application, charging new flight attendants for their uniforms, and charging tuition to attend the flight attendant training school. The airlines also started scheduling flights closer together so that a flight crew would have only a ten-hour layover between flights, instead of a twenty-four-hour respite. Competition among airlines mandated these changes, which led to higher productivity.

According to the Bureau of Labor Statistics, flight attendants jobs are expected to increase by 18.4 percent between 2000 and 2010. (This estimate was made prior to the events of September 11, 2001, when many flight attendants were furloughed.)

If travel and flexibility in your schedule are appealing to you, then flight attendant may be a good career choice. However, don't forget that there are drawbacks: within the first three years the pay is not favorable, and you will have little control over your schedule.

Pilots, Copilots, and Flight Engineers

According to the FAA, in 2001 there were 265,204 commercial and airline transport pilots and 65,398 flight engineers. Job prospects for major airlines are best for college graduates who have a commercial pilot's license or flight engineer's license and experience flying jets.

Job Responsibilities

A job whose glamour is equal to that of the flight attendant is airline pilot. In addition to their prestige, pilots are highly paid, up to $185,000 or more per year. The majority of pilots are captains, first officers (or copilots), and second officers (or flight engineers) who transport passengers and cargo. The rest are commercial pilots with flying responsibilities such as dusting crops, testing aircraft, tracking criminals, or monitoring traffic.

Pilot and Copilot

The commercial airline pilot arrives at the airport well before take-off time. After getting information from the meteorological office about weather conditions along the flight path, the pilot works out route, speed, and altitude in a conference with the airline dispatcher. He or she then coordinates this flight plan with the air traffic controllers. The copilot is generally with the pilot during these conferences and assists as requested in working out practical routes and altitudes.

They proceed to the airplane, where they check the controls, engines, and instruments, going down a long checklist item by item. Passengers board and are strapped in, the cabin-crew chief advises the pilot that they are ready, and the pilot obtains permission from air traffic control to taxi and then to take off. Once airborne, with the assistance of autopilot and the flight management computer, the pilots steer the plane along the planned route. The pilot or copilot makes frequent radio reports to controllers on the ground as to the plane's altitude, speed, and position; the weather; amount of fuel remaining; and anything unusual about the flight. Altitude and speed are changed, as well as the plane's heading, as the pilot deems necessary. Instruments detailing the condition of engines, amount of fuel, altitude, airspeed, and other factors are constantly scrutinized.

In case of an emergency, such as an engine becoming too hot or ice forming on the wings faster than it can be melted, the pilot must take time, distance, fuel, and other factors into consideration. Shutting down one engine, for example, will make it take longer to reach the destination. If low fog or clouds obscure the field at the destination, an approach on instruments may be necessary, with a controller on the ground "talking the plane down." Leaving the aircraft after the flight, the pilot and copilot must fill out records of the flight at the airline office before they have completed their day's work.

Some senior pilots become instructors. There is a considerable need for instructors because every time an airline starts using a new model of airplane, pilots must be taught how to fly it. Sometimes the first airline to start using a new model will instruct the pilots of several other airlines.

All categories of licenses require recency of experience. The FAA requires that pilots must pass a flight review with an instructor at least every two years. Pilots are often subject to unannounced spot checks by the FAA, and they must take regular six-month FAA/Transport Canada and company flight checks.

Not all pilots in the travel trade fly large passenger planes. Some of them are bush pilots who still "fly by the seat of their pants" to wilderness lakes, perhaps carrying a couple of fishermen whose canoe is lashed to the undercarriage of the floatplane. Skiers are borne to the tops of otherwise inaccessible mountains by helicopter or ski plane pilots, so they can ski down over miles of virgin snow. Single-engine aircraft tow gliders up three thousand or four thousand feet above ground level and release them to soar in the empyrean. Sport parachutists are taken aloft; then they jump out and aim for ground targets. Many pilots are employed by corporations to fly executives on business trips.

There are also many very small airlines, operating a few one- or two-engine planes to island resorts, offshore gambling havens, camps in the woods, and other places where there is a continuous but small stream of travelers. As an example, Scenic Airlines in Las Vegas flies tourists on a sightseeing trip to the Grand Canyon, lands them on the rim for a ground tour, and flies them back to Las Vegas at sunset. In such an operation, the pilot may conduct the ground tour, pick up the passengers from their hotels, and also perform the aircraft maintenance. He or she has considerable independence when airborne, but much less support from the ground than has the pilot of a commercial airline.

The actual minute-by-minute supervision of the aircraft in flight is not much work anymore. Whereas early pilots sometimes navigated by following highways and were lost when they got into fog, the modern pilot has all the advantages of radar and loran, radio compass, and many other helpful instruments. In addition, airline flight is monitored from the ground by flight controllers, who can advise pilots of the plane's precise position and warn about weather difficulties ahead, other aircraft in the path, or dangerously low altitude.

The pilot of past years controlled the plane's course constantly with a joystick; however, modern transport aircraft are flown mechanically during most of the flight, except during takeoff and landing. On most long flights, a minor compass correction once or twice an hour is about all that is needed to keep the aircraft in straight and level flight and on the shortest safe course to its destination. A computer makes all the tiny corrections that used to be made by a pilot's sensitive fingers on the joystick. But the pilot, copilot, and usually the flight engineer must be able to take control and fly the aircraft in any sort of emergency that might develop—from minor turbulence, to losing an engine, to diving the plane down to a safe altitude if the cabin is ruptured and depressurized.

Most of the pilot's skill and ability are never used, but are held in reserve in case of need. For people who want continual challenge to which they can respond vigorously, this kind of work can be frustrating. An airline pilot does not have the exciting fight against fate and elements that Charles Lindbergh had. Instead, he or she spends long hours just keeping an eye on things.

At the beginning and end of every flight, however, the pilot earns that high pay by lifting the monstrous machine into the air and bringing it safely back to earth. The pilot often is called the captain by the airlines. Like the captain of a ship, he or she has total responsibility for the safety of passengers, crew, and cargo. In the air, all passengers, as well as the flight crew, are subject to her or his orders. The copilot often is called first officer by the airlines, and the flight engineer second officer. In most airlines the captain wears four sleeve stripes, the first officer three, and the flight engineer two.

Work schedules are irregular, since they are based on when the majority of people want to fly. Vacationers typically want to fly on weekends and during nonbusiness hours. Airline pilots, on average, are away from home bases overnight about one-third of the time. Airlines provide them hotel rooms and expense allowances for this.

The Federal Aviation Act forbids airline pilots and copilots to fly more than 100 hours per month or 1,000 hours per year. Most of them fly about 75 hours a month, but total hours on duty, including layover time before return flights, usually rise to 120.

Most pilots and copilots enjoy liberal vacations and other fringe benefits, including a considerable amount of free or low-cost personal travel. Joining an airline's cockpit crew is difficult, and keeping the job is challenging, but the responsibility, pay, and prestige make it well worthwhile.

More and more women are becoming pilots, gaining experience, and flying hours as flying instructors and air-taxi pilots. In 2001 there were approximately 35,776 women pilots (students, private, commercial, airline transport, and other). The fact that the airlines prefer pilots with military training has made it difficult for women to break in, but as the military services admit more women to their flight programs, more women will also become airline pilots. (To find out more about female pilots, see the Sources of Information section at the end of this chapter.)

Flight Engineer

The flight engineer's job combines the fields of operations and maintenance of the aircraft. He or she is expected to be able to take over as captain of the plane if the pilot and copilot should in some way become disabled. Promotion to copilot comes after two to seven years and to pilot after five to fifteen years, in accordance with seniority and union contract.

New large aircraft have flight-management computers that do much of the flight engineer's work, so when they can safely do so, the airlines get along without flight engineers.

The main practical operating responsibility of the flight engineer is to know every blade and bolt and valve, every spark plug, transistor, wire, pipe, and tank on the aircraft. The flight engineer's place in the cockpit is well supplied with instruments that report on every critical point and phase of engine operation, electronic systems, fuel and its flow, temperature, and many other conditions.

When any instrument or combination of instruments shows something unusual, the flight engineer must be able to diagnose trouble rapidly, report it immediately to the pilot, and, if possible, repair it during the flight or arrange for removal of stress from an affected part until mechanics on the ground can repair it. If the next stop is at a small airport without mechanics trained for the particular type of aircraft, the flight engineer may well be the one to make the repair.

On a typical flight, the flight engineer joins the pilot and copilot in the preflight weather briefing and conference on route and altitude. Together they check the aircraft's maintenance record to be sure that needed overhauls and equipment replacement have been made as required. Arriving at the airplane, they inspect the exterior briefly, including the tires.

The flight engineer officer assists the pilot and copilot in making preflight checks of equipment, controls, and instruments in the cockpit. He or she checks fuel levels, electric power, and engine-report instruments. In flight, the flight engineer adjusts controls to keep the engines at maximum efficiency, records engine performance and fuel consumption at frequent intervals, and watches cabin pressure and temperature and adjusts them as necessary.

Requirements

There are four levels of pilot certificates: student, private, commercial, and air transport (U.S. terminology) or airline transport (Canadian terminology). We will address the last three categories.

All airline pilots must pass extensive physical health requirements. In the United States, medical certificates required by the Federal Aviation Administration (FAA) are categorized as first, second, or third class. In Canada, Transport Canada has category 1 or category 3 certificates. Each class or category has specific requirements, which are valid for varying lengths of time.

The minimum age for private pilot certification is seventeen years. The pilot must hold a valid third-class (U.S.) or category 3

(Canada) medical certificate. In addition to a basic education, he or she must have specialized instruction in areas such as aviation regulations, navigation, radio communications, weather observation and evaluation, aircraft loading, and flight planning; and must pass an FAA written examination and demonstration of flight planning and maneuvering.

For commercial pilot certification, the minimum age is eighteen years. The pilot must hold a valid and current second-class (U.S.) or category 1 (Canada) medical certificate. In addition to the education requirements of a private license, a pilot must have extensive aeronautical experience. This includes at least 250 hours of flight time (in Canada, 200 hours), plus a minimum of 100 hours as pilot-in-command, 50 hours of cross-country (20 hours in Canada), 10 hours of instrument instruction, and an instrument rating (in Canada an instrument rating is not required, but an applicant must have 20 hours of instrument time). For certification, the commercial pilot must pass a more stringent written examination and demonstration of FAA procedures than does a private pilot.

For air transport pilot certification, the minimum age is twenty-three years. The air transport pilot must hold a current and valid first-class (U.S.) or category 1 (Canada) medical certificate. For the United States, 1,500 flight hours (night and cross-country included) plus instrument rating are required. For Canada, a minimum of 1,500 flight hours (pilot-in-command and cross-country included) and a multi-engine rating in addition to an instrument rating are required. To be certified, air transport pilots must pass a more stringent written examination and demonstration of FAA procedures than do private or commercial pilots.

According to the FAA's Title 14 Code of Federal Regulations (CFR), Part 121—commonly known as the Age 60 Rule—a pilot may not engage in what are known as Part 121 operations if the pilot has reached age sixty. Part 121 covers scheduled passenger operations using multi-engine jet aircraft, scheduled passenger operations with multi-engine propeller airplanes that have a passenger seat configuration of ten or more seats, and common carriage operations of all-cargo airplanes that have a payload capacity of seventy-five hundred pounds or more. Pilots have been contesting the Age 60 Rule for years now.

For flight engineers, the same physical and height and weight standards are required by the airlines as for pilots and copilots—and the same coolness under fire. A flight engineer must be a high school graduate (some airlines require college as well) and must hold a valid and current second-class medical certificate in the United States. He or she is also required to have at least one of three aircraft ratings on the flight engineer certification as appropriate.

Education and Training

The armed forces have traditionally been an important source of training for many civilian pilots. Persons without armed forces training may become pilots by attending flight school. Most airlines require at least two years of college and prefer to hire college graduates.

As wars slip into history and time passes, the number of aviators with military training decreases. The FAA has certified some six hundred civilian flying schools to compensate for this. Among these are some colleges and universities that offer degree credit for pilot training. Airlines still prefer militarily trained pilots, but now they must also accept those with civilian training. The United States military has lost so many trained pilots to civilian work that it is hoping to curb this high attrition rate through special pay and bonuses. This will make the airlines more dependent upon civilian-trained aviators or on their own training for pilots and copilots.

Competition has been quite intense. Most of the candidates seeking employment possess a bachelor's degree and have jet or turboprop training and experience. Typically, they have well in excess of fifteen hundred total flight hours.

The major airlines strongly suggest getting a bachelor's degree, then joining the Air Force, Navy, Marines, or Army for flight training.

This is true throughout the airline industry. Learning to fly in a civilian flying school is possible but costly, and it could be difficult to acquire the fifteen hundred hours of flight time required for the transport license. In time of war, when the military is using all the pilots it can get, the airline industry would no doubt take new pilots with minimum qualifications or even less than minimum. But during times of peace, when there are thousands of pilots looking for flying jobs, the airlines can take their pick, and they naturally choose the most highly qualified.

A sample description for a pilot's job with a major airline reads something like this:

> The minimum qualifications required for pilot are: being at least twenty-one years of age and a graduate of a four-year degree program from a college or university accredited by a recognized accrediting organization. Postgraduate education will be given favorable consideration. Applicants should currently hold an FAA commercial fixed-wing pilot license with an instrument rating; currently hold a valid FAA second-officer written exam (FEB and FEJ or FEX); and have a minimum of 1,200 hours of total documented flight time with a minimum of 1,000 hours of fixed-wing turboprop or turbofan time. Applicants invited to interview must provide

appropriate documentation of all flight hours and possess a current FAA First Class Medical Certificate and be able to pass a medical examination. Part of the pre-employment screening process will require applicants to take a test to determine the presence (without a prescription) in the applicant's system of any substance that is controlled in the United States. Applicants must be able to pass a criminal and background check in order to qualify for unrestricted access to security identification display areas; possess a valid passport or other travel documents enabling the bearer to freely exit and re-enter the United States (multiple re-entry status); and be legally eligible to work in the United States (possess proper working documents).

Before being allowed to take up passengers, the newly hired flight engineer, copilot, or pilot is given extensive training by the airline. This includes classroom instruction in meteorology, FAA regulations, and company policies and rules. Three to ten weeks of flight instruction consisting of lectures, time in simulated aircraft, and actual flights may also be given. A trainee who does not have a rating for the type of airplane he or she will be flying must earn it.

Very few people are hired to start as pilot/captain for the major airlines. Historically, most began as second officers, with eventual promotion to first officer and finally to captain. Nowadays, however, as second officers are being replaced by new technology, one's first job on the flight deck is as first officer. Reaction time and ability to make rapid correct judgments under stress are tested, and cockpit crew members must maintain excellent physical condition to keep their jobs.

Safe flying is the major ability demanded by airlines of their pilots. Punctuality for on-time departures and arrivals also is desirable, but safety is always paramount. Heroes are really not desired in this job. Airlines prefer steady, eminently well-qualified people who take pride in their own perfectionism as they check out equipment, weather, and all the many items that might possibly go wrong and cause trouble during flight. In addition to being a perfectionist, a pilot must be cool in emergencies. Previous flying experience, often in the military, will probably have subjected the pilot to many emergencies, perhaps in combat, where her or his mettle was tested and proved.

The best way for flight engineers to obtain the necessary training is in the armed forces, just as for pilots and copilots. A FAA flight engineer license is required. Qualification for this consists of three or more years of experience as a pilot or second officer in the armed forces, or in repair and overhaul of aircraft engines. A stiff flight physical examination and a written test on engine operation and the theory of flight are also required for this license, plus a flight check in an aircraft of the type to which the engineer seeks assignment. An applicant without armed services experience can study for the license at a private aviation school approved by the FAA. Also required is the commercial pilot's license.

Earnings and Job Outlook

In 2000, the average salary for airline pilots, copilots, and flight engineers was $110,940. According to a September 2001 report from the Air Lines Pilots Association, International (ALPA), which represents sixty-six thousand airline pilots from United States and Canadian airlines, ALPA captains earned an average of $150,000. ALPA copilots earned an average of $93,000 annually. For airlines that do not fly aircraft requiring three crew members in the cockpit, the starting salary for a copilot ranged from $17,500 to $50,000 annually. ALPA flight engineers earned an average of

$85,000 annually, and entry-level salaries ranged from $36,000 to $50,000.

Airline pilots and copilots earn more than those employed by corporations or government. More than half of U.S. airline pilots are members of a union. Most who fly for one of the major airlines belong to the Air Line Pilots Association, International. The union representing Air Canada's pilots is the Canadian Air Line Pilots Association. Pilot pay is decided upon by bargaining between union and company.

The Bureau of Labor Statistics reported that 94,820 pilots were employed in 2000. Air travel is very sensitive to economic swings, however, and a recession always causes reduction in numbers of flights and consequent crew layoffs. Restructuring of airlines in the 1990s and the events of September 11, 2001, have reduced the need for pilots.

According to the Bureau of Labor Statistics, jobs for pilots, copilots, and flight engineers are expected to increase by 6.4 percent between 2000 and 2010. (This estimate was made prior to September 11, 2001, when many pilots, copilots, and flight attendants were furloughed.)

Aircraft Mechanics

One way in which a person can prepare to become a flight engineer is to first become an aircraft mechanic. There are almost twice as many aircraft mechanics as there are pilots, copilots, and flight engineers combined. Although the traveling public seldom sees aircraft mechanics, there would be no flying without them.

In 2000, 173,000 aircraft mechanics were employed in the United States. Approximately 70 percent of all salaried mechanics worked for airlines or airports and flying fields, about 12 percent worked for the federal government, and about 9 percent worked for aircraft assembly firms. Many of the remaining mechanics worked in general aviation, usually for independent repair shops. Many who work for the aircraft assembly firms are in California or Washington state. FAA facilities are in Oklahoma City; Atlanta; Wichita; or Washington, D.C. An airline usually operates a major repair base for each type of aircraft in its system.

Job Responsibilities

There are three main specialties among aircraft mechanics: power plant, airframe, and avionics technicians. Avionics technicians work on instruments and propellers. Airframe mechanics are qualified to work on wings, fuselages, and landing gear, while power plant mechanics work on engines.

In addition to doing such routine preventive maintenance as changing engine oil, greasing wheel bearings, and replacing spark plugs, aircraft mechanics dismantle engines, check all the parts for wear, and rebuild them. The FAA requires regular inspection of airframes and power plants. When a flight is delayed for emergency repairs, mechanics must work fast to get the plane back into the air.

Education and Training

Training for most mechanics consists of graduation from high school or vocational school, plus some experience in a machine shop or auto repair shop. Major airlines operate apprenticeship programs of three or four years' duration, combining classroom and on-the-job training. Those who have been aircraft mechanics in the armed forces can complete their apprenticeship rapidly. Or, if they are fortunate enough to have worked with aircraft very similar to those the airline flies, they might step right into a mechanic's job. The FAA has a list of mechanic schools that it has approved, and it will make the list available to anyone who is interested. Programs at most of these schools are of one and a half to two years' duration.

Graduates of these schools, or mechanics with eighteen months of experience, are eligible to take the written and practical tests for a license as an airframe or power plant mechanic or as an avionics repair specialist (A & P specialist). A mechanic trying for both airframe and power plant licenses at once must have thirty months of experience. A mechanic who has had both licenses for at least three years may take examinations and be qualified as an aircraft inspector, after which he or she certifies the work of other mechanics.

Licensed mechanics advance with increasing seniority and ability to lead. A mechanic may become a crew chief, shop foreman, maintenance supervisor, and perhaps company executive. Some start their own shops and work on contract for small airlines, corporations, government agencies, or other general aviation aircraft operators. Others learn to fly well enough to earn a commercial pilot's license and become flight engineers.

Earnings and Job Outlook

The airlines paid aircraft and service technicians an average of $19.50 an hour in 2000. Avionics technicians were paid an average of $19.86 per hour. Mechanics who are employed by the major airlines generally earn more than those working on other types of aircraft do. In addition, aircraft mechanics and technicians with FAA certification earn on average more than $4.00 per hour over those who are not FAA-certified.

Free or low-cost travel on the mechanic's own and other airlines, plus other fringe benefits, are standard.

Unions representing aircraft mechanics include the International Association of Machinists and Aerospace Workers, the Transport Workers Union of America, and the International Brotherhood of Teamsters.

Although employment of aircraft mechanics is expected to rise with the average for all occupations through the year 2010, it may be restricted as consolidation in the aircraft industry continues and more and more automated systems take on tasks for repair and replacement in aircraft. According to the Bureau of Labor Statistics, jobs for aircraft mechanics are expected to increase by 16.7 percent between 2000 and 2010.

Air Traffic Controllers

The FAA was the employer of twenty-seven thousand air traffic controllers in 2000. Most air traffic controllers are stationed in the towers at major airports, at en route centers along established airways, or at flight service stations near large cities. Some work for the United States Department of Defense.

Heavy responsibility puts air traffic controllers under great stress, so anyone entering this kind of work should be prepared to cope with extremes of tension over long hours. Controllers may retire on pension after twenty to twenty-five years—a recognition of the strain they undergo. Mandatory retirement is at fifty-six years of age, and the National Air Traffic Controllers Association estimates half of the nation's controllers will retire by 2010, necessitating the hiring of new controllers to fill the positions.

Job Responsibilities

There are three types of air traffic control specialists (ATCS)—the terminal (or tower) controller, en route center controller, and the flight-service station controller—and their main responsibility is to ensure the safe, orderly flow of air traffic. The terminal controller's main responsibility is to organize the flow of aircraft in and out of the airport. The en route controller takes over when an aircraft leaves an airport, directing pilots through their designated airspace. A flight-service specialist provides pilots with flight and in-flight weather information, suggested routes, and other important flight information.

Education and Training

Applicants for American controller duties must be U.S. citizens, younger than thirty-one years of age, have vision correctable to 20/20, and have clear, precise diction. Many controllers come from the armed forces, while many others are trained by FAA-certified colleges with degrees in aviation administration with an emphasis in air traffic control. Applicants usually must have three years of general work experience or four years of college or a combination of both. The United States Office of Personnel Management gives competitive examinations in major American cities.

Chosen applicants are given eleven to sixteen weeks of classroom and on-the-job training at the FAA Air Traffic Academy in Oklahoma City. They learn aircraft performance characteristics, aviation regulations, the airways system, and controller equipment, and receive intensive training in flight simulators. Full qualification as a controller takes three to six years. Every controller is given a physical examination once a year and a job performance review twice a year. Controllers can advance to chief controller, regional controller, and to administrative positions in the FAA.

Control towers never close down, so controllers must work frequent night shifts on a rotating basis. In addition to their forty-hour workweek, they may work extra hours for overtime pay or compensatory time off.

Earnings and Job Outlook

According to the Bureau of Labor Statistics, the average annual salary in 2000 was $53,313. The middle 50 percent earned between $62,250 and $101,570, the lowest 10 percent earned less than $44,760, and the highest 10 percent earned more than $111,150. The government gives thirteen to twenty-six paid vacation days and thirteen days of sick leave annually. Controllers' salaries are determined by collective bargaining contracts. The trade union is the National Air Traffic Controllers Association.

According to the Bureau of Labor Statistics, jobs for air traffic controllers are expected to increase by 7.2 percent between 2000 and 2010.

Further information and application forms are available from the U.S. Office of Personnel Management (see the Sources of Information section at the end of this chapter), which also administers the written test.

Aviation Safety Inspectors

The FAA is responsible for the safety of almost every facet of aviation, including certification of aircraft, pilots, mechanics, and people involved in manufacturing aircraft. In 2001 U.S. aviation was serving more than 622 million passengers, a number expected to rise to one billion by 2013, according to the FAA.

Job Responsibilities

Aviation safety inspectors administer and enforce safety regulations and standards for the production, operation, maintenance, and/or modification of aircraft used in civil aviation. There are eight different types of FAA inspectors, including (1–3) general aviation avionics/maintenance/operations inspectors; (4–6) air carrier avionics/maintenance/operations inspectors; (7) manufacturing inspectors; and (8) cabin inspectors.

Requirements

Experience is the primary requirement for an inspector's job. For example, candidates for a manufacturing inspector position must have experience in the area of quality control/quality assurance systems, methods, and the techniques in the manufacture of aircraft, aircraft engines, propellers, or class II products. This experience should demonstrate their ability to determine that aircraft and related products meet the approved design criteria and are in condition for safe operation. They may also have responsibility for the issuance of original airworthiness certificates or original expert airworthiness approvals for aircraft, aircraft engines, propellers, and class II products.

Avionics, maintenance, operations, and manufacturing inspectors are hired primarily from a national registry or pool of qualified applications. An application must be filled out, and an applicant is notified if he or she is eligible for an inspector position. For cabin safety inspectors, if a vacancy is available, it is posted on the FAA Career Opportunities website (see the Sources of Information section at the end of this chapter).

Earnings and Job Outlook

U.S. Aviation Safety Inspector (ASI) earnings are classified according to the General Schedule (GS) pay tables and range from GS-9 (2002 tables: $43,365) to GS-15 (2002 tables: $104,604). Current GS pay tables can be obtained from the U.S. Office of Personnel Management (OPM) website. (See the Sources of Information section at the end of this chapter). Earnings in the Washington, D.C., headquarters area generally range from GS-12 to GS-15.

The FAA continues to look for people who are technically proficient with the emerging aviation technologies, have strong business systems management skills, and are competent in the use and application of information technology.

Reservation and Transportation Agents and Travel Clerks

In 2000, according to the Bureau of Labor Statistics, 126,000 people held jobs as reservation and transportation agents and travel clerks in the air transportation industry.

Job Responsibilities

Reservation agents and clerks for major airlines and large hotel chains generally work in central offices. As the human link between the telephone and a computer terminal, the agent gives information on flight schedules and the availability of seats and makes reservations. Agents receive calls from the general public, from travel agents, and from their own company's ticket agents. They generally do not come face-to-face with customers, but do all their contact work by telephone.

Transportation agents, sometimes known as passenger service agents, passenger-booking clerks, reservations clerks, airport service agents, or ticket clerks, work at ticket counters in airports and in central-city ticket offices. They answer questions about fares and schedules, give out timetables and descriptive literature, check directly with computers or with reservation agents for seat availability, and sell tickets, often by typing the passengers' names into the computer. Fares are so complicated in air travel that selling a ticket is a more difficult procedure than it might seem. Ticket agents check in and tag baggage, add any excess-baggage charges, and issue boarding passes to permit passengers to get to the airplanes. Passenger agents help airport ticket agents, help passengers board the aircraft, collect tickets, and in some cases assign seats. At some airlines, these personnel are called customer service clerks (entry level) and customer service agents.

Ticket and passenger agents are as smartly uniformed as flight crews. They are selected on the basis of pleasing personality and appearance, good diction, and education. High school graduation generally is required, and two or more years of college are preferred. Chances for advancement are improved by college courses in traffic management and other phases of transportation.

Outside sales agents for the airlines often are called traffic representatives. They visit shippers and corporations, keeping present customers happy and trying to obtain new customers. Ticket and reservation agents may advance to supervisor in these specialties or to traffic representative.

Heading all sales efforts are city sales managers, and above them, district sales managers. The district sales manager administers ticket and reservations offices, directs the efforts of sales representatives, and promotes traffic on the airline.

Earnings and Job Outlook

According to the Bureau of Labor Statistics, the median hourly earnings for reservation and transportation agents and travel clerks in 2000 were $11.67. As automated reservations—such as "ticketless" travel or kiosks to let passengers book their own flights—reduce the number of workers necessary, job outlook for these types of positions will not rise significantly. However, travel-related positions can never be fully automated for security and safety reasons, and as travel grows and turnover in the industry occurs, there will be job openings.

According to the Bureau of Labor Statistics, jobs for reservation and transportation ticket agents and travel clerks are expected to increase by 14.5 percent between 2000 and 2010.

Sources of Information

The many organizations associated with the airline industry have excellent sources of information, including up-to-date job websites. Here are some:

Air Line Pilots Association, International (ALPA)
1625 Massachusetts Ave. NW
Washington, DC 20036-2283
alpa.org

Career information, including a list of accredited pilot schools in the United States and Canada, can be found at: alpa.org/internet/ publications/cpb/career_pilot_brochure.pdf.

ALPA is a union representing sixty-six thousand airline pilots at forty-three U.S. and Canadian airlines. Founded in 1931, it is chartered by the AFL-CIO.

Air Transport Association, Inc. (ATA)
1301 Pennsylvania Ave. NW, #1100
Washington, DC 20004
airlines.org

ATA is the nation's largest airline trade association, accounting for 95 percent of the passenger and cargo traffic carried by U.S. scheduled airlines.

Association of Flight Attendants, AFL-CIO (AFA)
1275 K St. NW
Washington, DC 20005
afanet.org

Career information is available at: afanet.org/airline_job_links.htm. AFA is the world's largest labor union organized by flight attendants for flight attendants. It represents more than fifty thousand flight attendants at twenty-six airlines.

Aviation Information Resources, Inc. (AIR, Inc.)
3800 Camp Creek Pkwy., Ste. 18-100
Atlanta, GA 30331
airapps.com

AIR is dedicated to providing complete, timely, and accurate information to help pilots make informed decisions throughout their job search and to assist them in their career development as airline pilots.

Federal Aviation Administration (FAA)
U.S. Department of Transportation
800 Independence Ave. SW
Washington, DC 20591
faa.gov
FAA Aviation Education Career Guides: faa.gov/education/rlib/
career.htm
FAA approved air traffic controller schools: faa.gov/education/rlib/
atc.htm
FAA Air Traffic Academy website: atctraining.faa.gov/site

International Flight Engineers' Organization (IFEO)
IFALPA Headquarters
Interpilot House
Chertsey, UK KT16 9AP
ifalpa.org

IFEO was formed in 1992 by the merger of the Flight Engineers' International Association (FEIA) and the European Flight Engineers Organization (EFEO). It is now the only international organization for flight engineers.

International Society of Women Airline Pilots (ISA+21)
2250-E Tropicana Ave., Ste. 19-395
Las Vegas, NV 89119-6594
iswap.org

ISA+21 is an educational and charitable nonprofit organization that seeks to stimulate and encourage women to enter the airline pilot workforce as active cockpit crew via education and scholarship.

National Air Traffic Controllers Association (NATCA)
1325 Massachusetts Ave.
Washington, DC 20005
natca.org

NATCA ensures the safety and longevity of air traffic controller positions around the nation.

The Ninety-Nines, Inc.
International Organization of Women Pilots
International Headquarters
Box 965, 7100 Terminal Dr.
Oklahoma City, OK 73159-0965
ninety-nines.org

The Ninety-Nines is an international organization of licensed women pilots from thirty-five countries and has more than sixty-five hundred members worldwide.

Professional Aviation Maintenance Association (PAMA)
Ronald Reagan Washington National Airport
Washington, DC 20001
pama.org

PAMA's mission is to enhance professionalism and recognition of the aviation maintenance technician through communication, education, representation, and support for continuous improvement in aviation safety.

Transport Canada
Department of Transport
330 Sparks St.
Ottawa, ON
Canada K1A 0N5
tc.gc.ca

Transport Canada works to help ensure Canadians the best transportation system by developing and administering policies, regulations, and programs for a safe, efficient, and environmentally friendly transportation system.

Universal Pilot Application Service (UPAS)
P.O. Box 550010
Ft. Lauderdale, FL 33355-0010
upas.com

U.S. Bureau of Labor Statistics (BLS)
U.S. Department of Labor
2 Massachusetts Ave. NE
Washington, DC 20212-0001
bls.gov

U.S. Bureau of Transportation Statistics (BTS)
U.S. Department of Transportation
400 Seventh St. SW
Washington, DC 20590
bts.gov

U.S. Department of Transportation (DOT)
400 Seventh St. SW
Washington, DC 20590
dot.gov

U.S. Office of Personnel Management (OPM)
1900 E St. NW
Washington, DC 20415-0001
opm.gov
Job openings: usajobs.opm.gov
GS pay tables: opm.gov/oca/02tables/indexgs.htm

This is the human resources agency of the U.S. government.

3

CRUISE LINES, RAILROADS, AND BUS LINES

THE AIRLINE INDUSTRY has grown to be a gigantic industry in the last two decades, overshadowing other modes of travel such as boat, rail, and bus. However, there are many places that airplanes cannot get to, and the alternative method of getting there would be by railroad and bus. Travel by boat—including cruise ships, car and passenger ferries, excursion and dinner boats, and gaming vessels—is expanding in the United States as the demand for waterborne recreation grows and federal, state, and local governments find ways to ease congestion on highways and roads. There are many job opportunities for those interested in working in the travel industry in these fields. This chapter includes information on the historical background, job responsibilities, training, earnings, and job outlook and information resources of the cruise, rail, and bus industries.

Cruise Lines

According to the Cruise Lines International Association (CLIA), the cruise industry is the fastest-growing segment of the travel industry—achieving more than 1,400 percent growth since 1970, when approximately 500,000 people took a cruise. It is estimated that by 2002, 7.4 million people will have taken a cruise.

The North American cruise industry's growth is also reflected in the significant increase in passenger capacity. In the 1990s, nearly eighty new ships were introduced, and over the next five years, the cruise industry will introduce at least fifty-two new ships. Furthermore, in North America, only 12.3 percent of the population has ever taken a cruise, and polls suggest that over 50 percent would like to.

About two-thirds of the world's cruise trade is generated in the North American market, but most cruise-ship officers are European, while most crew members are European, West Indian, or Asian.

The cruise industry is an important part of the U.S. travel industry. According to a study conducted by Business Research and Economic Advisors (BREA) and Wharton Econometric Forecasting Association (WEFA), the cruise industry contributed some $17.9 billion to the U.S. economy in 2000 and generated 257,000 full-time jobs for U.S. citizens.

There are few American cruise ships or freighters. The United States Merchant Marine has been in sad straits for years because of the cost of American labor, both for building ships and for staffing them. Costs are three or four times what ship owners in Europe and Asia pay. As a consequence, U.S. shipping survives only when heavily subsidized by the government or when heavy defense spending for military or aid ventures brings employment to American ships. Congress in 1970 agreed to subsidize the construction of thirty new ships per year until 1980. This vigorous construction program was intended to revitalize American shipping, but in actual practice, older ships were retired or scrapped at the same rate new ones were built.

Many U.S. shipping companies register their ships in Panama, Liberia, and other countries where they can pay low taxes and avoid high labor rates. Americans can work on these ships, but at low rates of pay. Also, having worked on a ship flying a "flag of convenience," an American may have a difficult time later getting a job on an American-flag ship, because a U.S. union might refuse membership.

Passenger transportation across the oceans has been taken over almost completely by the airlines, and the great passenger liners have been retired or adapted to the cruise trade. Cruising has been gaining rapidly in popularity, and it is the salvation of the passenger ship. Many new cruise ships were built in the 1980s, and about twenty were under construction in 1995. New York City, formerly the departure point for about one hundred cruises to the Caribbean every winter, built a new passenger ship terminal in 1974. Fly-cruise packages had been introduced, however, giving the passenger a flight to meet a ship in Miami or a Caribbean port; this gradually ended winter cruises from New York. But as more and more people discovered the delights of the cruise, the cruise season became a year-round industry in the Caribbean.

From New York City, beginning in the mid-1980s, some three hundred cruises departed annually during warm weather, sailing to Bermuda, the Bahamas, Canada, and all around the Caribbean. Cruises up the inland waterway to Alaska and from West Coast ports to Mexico, Central and South America, and the Caribbean are also increasing their sailings and bookings. Fly-cruise packages now also take North Americans to join their ships in the Mediterranean, in Hawaii, and in the Orient.

Job Responsibilities

If you think of a cruise ship as a ship, hotel, theater, entertainment center, sports center, wellness spa, restaurant, bar, shopping mall, and many other types of businesses combined, you can imagine the varying types of jobs on board. Job titles range from beautician, cashier, and cruise or recreation director to nurse and doctor. Bartender, purser, and tour staff are popular jobs, but oftentimes one must start out as a room steward (or stewardess) and work up to waiter, bartender, or office staff.

Careers at sea in the "water transportation industry" are still possible for Americans on American- or foreign-flag ships and even in the United States passenger trade. According to the Bureau of Labor Statistics, there were 70,000 water transportation workers in 2000. This figure includes 32,000 sailor and marine oilers, 25,000 ship and boat captains and operators, and 8,600 ship engineers.

Shipboard work is divided among three departments. The deck department operates and navigates the ship, maintains the hull and deck equipment, and supervises loading, storing, and unloading of cargo. The engine department operates and maintains the propulsive machinery. And finally, the steward's department feeds the crew and passengers and cleans the living spaces.

Education and Training

It is possible to become captain of a ship with no formal education. The catch is that there are many Coast Guard examinations to take to qualify for the licenses that are necessary to advance. The person with no educational background is up against severe competition from graduates of the one federal and six state merchant marine academies.

To do it the hard way, one would obtain seaman's papers from the Coast Guard, wait in a union hiring hall until shipped out as an ordinary seaman, after a year take examinations to become an able seaman, after three years at sea take examinations for third mate, and at annual intervals take examinations for second mate and master status. However, this progression would take many years, and even with master's papers, the seaman might not always become captain of a ship.

A more likely path to advancement is graduation from the United States Merchant Marine Academy at Kings Point, New York, or one of the six state maritime academies. Like the service academies, entrance to the United States Merchant Marine Academy is by congressional appointment and College Entrance Board examinations. Students are paid a small allowance, and their education is free. The second year is spent at sea aboard an American commercial ship. Each graduate receives a Bachelor of Science degree, a license as third mate or third assistant engineer, and an ensign's commission in the United States Naval Reserve. Almost without exception, this is the course followed by prospective ship captains today. The law requires that graduates of the Merchant Marine Academy must serve at least five years in the merchant marine or the military.

The Merchant Marine Academy places nearly all its graduates in seagoing jobs before they graduate. Merchant marine officers' careers from that point depend upon their doing a good job, studying for examinations for second mate and master, and taking the exams as early as possible. After this, they simply must work and wait for a captain's job.

The six state academies are: California Maritime Academy at Vallejo; Maine Maritime Academy at Castine; Massachusetts Maritime Academy at Buzzards Bay; Texas Maritime Academy at Galveston; New York Maritime College at Fort Schuyler, New York City; and Great Lakes Maritime Academy at Traverse City, Michigan. All these schools charge tuition. Contact the Office of Maritime Labor and Training (see the Sources of Information following this section) for a list of the state maritime academies and the link to the United States Merchant Marine Academy.

People in the steward's department generally work up from unskilled jobs such as mess attendant and utility hand to third cook, second cook (the ship's baker), and chief cook. Above the chief cook is the chief steward. The chief steward is not a ship's officer, but nevertheless is answerable to the captain. On a passenger ship, the steward's department is by far the largest, employing many waiters and room stewards.

When doing job research, it's wise to determine the nationality of the ship's crew. Often it is difficult to get an engine room or desk job unless you are the same nationality as the ship's officers. Most ship's officers are Norwegian, Greek, or Italian, with a handful of British and American ships. In addition, many of the technical crew jobs in the engine room or on deck are staffed with Filipinos.

It is best to go directly to the cruise lines when seeking employment for a position other than captain, ship engineer, or sailor. For a list of all cruise ships' mailing and website addresses, log on to the Cruise Lines International Association (CLIA) or the International Council of Cruise Lines (ICCL) websites listed in the Sources of Information at the end of this section.

Earnings and Job Outlook

According to the Bureau of Labor Statistics in 2000, water transportation earnings varied considerably by position and experience, from minimum wage to $33.77 per hour for a ship engineer position. Median hourly earnings for ship or boat captains and operators were $21.62; ship engineers, $22.85; sailor and marine oilers, $13.52; and all other types of positions, $11.70.

Shipboard personnel receive free room and board, so they are able to save most of their earnings if they can withstand the temptations of the ports they visit. Premium rates are paid for overtime. Officers generally can earn about 50 percent above base pay for overtime and extra responsibilities. There are numerous strong unions covering most seafaring jobs.

In a 2000 cruise market study by the Cruise Lines International Association, it was found that the existing cumulative market potential over the next five years could be as high as $85 billion, creating the need for personnel growth. According to the Bureau of Labor Statistics, jobs for ship and boat captains and operators are expected to increase by 3.4 percent between 2000 and 2010, and 5.8 percent for ship engineers.

Sources of Information

Canadian Merchant Service Guild
218 Blue Mountain St., Ste. 310
Coquitlam, BC
Canada V3K 4H2

Cruise Lines International Association (CLIA)
500 Fifth Ave., Ste. 1407
New York, NY 10110
cruising.org

CLIA is the official trade organization of the North American cruise industry.

International Council of Cruise Lines (ICCL)
2111 Wilson Blvd., 8th Fl.
Arlington, VA 22201
iccl.org

The ICCL's mission is to participate in the regulatory and policy development process and promote all measures that foster a safe, secure, and healthy cruise ship environment.

International Organization of Masters, Mates, and Pilots
700 Maritime Blvd.
Linthicum Heights, MD 21090
bridgedeck.org

Marine Engineers' Beneficial Association
444 N. Capitol St., Ste. 800
Washington DC 20001
d1meba.org

Office of Maritime Labor and Training
Maritime Administration
U.S. Department of Transportation
400 Seventh St. SW
Washington, DC 20590
marad.dot.gov

Paul Hall Center of Maritime Training and Education
P.O. Box 75
Piney Point, MD 20674-0075
seafarers.org/phc

Seafarers' International Union of North America
5201 Auth Way
Camp Springs, MD 20746
seafarers.org

U.S. Coast Guard National Maritime Center
Licensing and Evaluation Branch
4200 Wilson Blvd., Ste. 630
Arlington, VA 22203-1804
uscg.mil/stcw/m-pers.htm

Railroads

Following World War II, the airlines gradually took over most of the long-haul domestic passenger traffic that traditionally had belonged to the railroads. Service on many lines became so poor that it seemed the railroads were trying to get rid of passengers. As new population centers developed, there were many places not served by rail, and no new rail lines were laid. Intercity bus service improved and carried most of those passengers who did not fly or use their own cars. By 1970, railroads were accounting for only 1 percent of intercity passenger miles.

A new chapter in railroad history began when the National Railroad Passenger Corporation (Amtrak)—a quasi-public corporation dedicated to providing modern, efficient, attractive service—began operating the nation's passenger railroads on May 1,

1971. Amtrak was started just in time. It finally had been admitted that automobiles were a prime cause of air pollution and that individual transportation would have to be reduced by improving mass transportation, which causes less pollution. Then came the energy crisis of the winter of 1973–74, reinforced in the spring of 1979, which jolted Americans into realizing that a really severe shortage of gasoline could force them to use mass transportation.

There were many growing pains as Amtrak strove to meet rapidly increasing demands. New types of trains were designed and built, many cars were bought, and a nationwide computerized ticketing and reservation system was installed and operating in 1974. Many of the roadbeds were in poor repair, and introduction of high-speed trains was pointless until the roadbeds were improved. Amtrak improved the New York–Washington tracks so that fast metroliners could travel at 110 miles per hour. An investment that has paid off splendidly is America's first high-speed train, the Acela Express, in the Northeast corridor. It is now constantly full with passengers, it cost less than $3 billion all told, and, as of this date, it is operating in the black. Washington and Oregon are spending state money to build a high-speed corridor between Seattle and Portland. In Chicago, a liberal nonprofit law firm is spearheading a nine-state high-speed effort for the Midwest United States.

Amtrak has been very heavily subsidized by congressional appropriations since its inception. In 1979 Congress mandated that Amtrak be able to pay its own way by the end of 2002, which it has not been able to do. Amtrak asked for a loan of $205 million in short-term financial help, threatening to shut down the passenger rail lines and the commuter lines that use its tracks at the end of June 2002. Negotiations took place in the summer of 2002. Legislators were leaning toward liquidating Amtrak and returning the rails to private service. However, just as the deadline was approaching, Congress agreed once more to bail out Amtrak. To date, Amtrak's financial problems are not yet resolved.

Canada's rail history has been similar to that of the United States, with passengers leaving the railroads to drive their own cars, and equipment and tracks sinking into poor condition. Equipment and maintenance improvements have been made, but at high cost. The Canadian government contributed $597 million for 1983 expenses in excess of revenue. The ongoing improvements the Canadian Rail System (VIA) achieved over the past decade continued in 2001. Revenue increased by $13 million, bringing total revenue growth over the last three years to more than $50 million. Passenger numbers increased by seventy thousand and yield—the measure of revenue earned per passenger mile—increased by approximately 6 percent. Despite higher fuel costs, total operating costs were lower than anticipated. As a result, VIA was able to reduce its requirement for government operating funding by another $7 million. And for the first time in VIA's history, the ratio of revenues over cash operating expenses exceeded 60 percent to reach 61.5 percent.

The U.S. Department of Labor noted 531,000 railroaders working in 1976, 433,000 in 1982, and 115,000 in 2000. Railroad jobs, as expected, continued declining at a rate of 1.8 percent a year.

Job Responsibilities

There are a number of important jobs involved in rail travel. They include the following:

Clerks

Clerks are the largest group of railroad employees. They work in railroad stations, company offices, yards, terminals, and freight houses. Most railroads require a high school education and may require applicants to take a clerical aptitude test. Some clerical training or experience also is beneficial. Most clerks belong to the Transportation Communications International Union. Railroad clerks can advance in many directions—to cashier, executive secretary, accountant, statistician, chief clerk, auditor, ticket agent, station agent, buyer, or supervisor. Both men and women have found opportunities in this area.

All passenger rail systems, including Amtrak, utilize a nationwide computerized reservation system, an innovation in passenger railroading. Most passengers now get information through computerized telephone lines and can book their own reservations online. This has resulted in the decrease in the number of clerks needed to handle reservations and information.

Conductors

The conductor is in charge of the train, whether it carries freight or passengers. He or she signals the engineer when to start, and can order a stop for any emergency. Passenger-train conductors collect tickets and money and furnish schedule and fare information.

Conductors are usually male and are promoted from the job of brake operator, which used to be called brakeman or trainman. Passenger-service brake operators attend to car lighting and temperature and may help collect tickets. Many women are now passenger-service brake operators, and many of them will become conductors.

Conductors, brake operators, and all train-crew personnel often work irregular hours, including nights and weekends, getting premium pay for overtime. Most brake operators and conductors belong to the United Transportation Union.

Engineers and Brake Operators

Locomotive engineers drive great machines powered by diesel engines or electricity. They are the most experienced and skilled workers on the railroad. A few people are hired specifically for training to become engineers; most are promoted from brake operator positions after passing examinations.

Newly hired brake operators should be between the ages of twenty-one and thirty-five, with a high school education and excellent hearing, eyesight, color vision, and hand-eye coordination.

The new brake operator is trained on-the-job by the engineers with whom he or she rides and is given a regular assignment when one becomes available. Within a year of being hired, the helper starts a six-month engineer-training course, which is composed of both formal instruction and on-the-job training. He or she must pass numerous tests to qualify as an engineer, and then may have to wait several years until there is a vacancy. In passenger service, brake operators are often called assistant conductors.

Shift work is common in over-the-road work and in local lines and yards.

Station Agents

Station agents in small stations sell tickets, check baggage, compute express and freight charges, and may direct the operation of some trains. In progressively larger stations, the station agent is a supervisor of these activities or an administrator of a large staff.

Station agents usually are promoted from the ranks of railroad clerks, telegraphers, telephoners, and tower operators. Those in the last three groups direct the movement of trains from towers in terminals and yards. To be hired, they should be high school graduates and have excellent hearing, eyesight, color vision, and diction.

Amtrak wants its employees to advance and has a program to provide educational assistance for employees who want to take job-related courses of study. There is also a very liberal pass policy at Amtrak and on most nonpassenger railroad lines. Amtrak employees have unlimited free transportation on a space-available basis, excluding certain special high-fare trains. Employees' spouses and dependents are given twelve free trips a year and as many more as they desire at half fare.

Earnings and Job Outlook

According to the Bureau of Labor Statistics, median hourly earnings of locomotive engineers were $21.26 in 2000; railroad conductors and yardmasters, $18.86; railroad brake, signal, and switch operators, $18.82; and rail yard engineers, dinkey operators, and hostlers, $17.69.

Most railroad workers in road service are paid according to miles traveled or hours worked, whichever leads to higher earnings. Full-time employees have steadier work, more regular hours, increased opportunities for overtime work, and higher earnings than do those assigned to the "extra" board.

According to the National Railroad Labor Conference (NRLC), in 1999 the average annual earnings for Class I railroad engineers ranged from $61,400 for yard-freight engineers to $81,000 for passenger engineers. For conductors, earnings ranged from $53,500 for yard-freight conductors up to $68,300 for passenger conductors. The NRLC reported that brake operators averaged from $40,800 for yard-freight operators up to $58,700 for local-freight operators.

According to data from the American Public Transportation Association, in early 2001 the top-rate full-time hourly earnings of operators for commuter rail ranged from $17.50 to $30.10; operators for heavy rail from $16.20 to $27.70; and operators for light rail from $14.40 to $23.90. Transit workers in the northeastern United States typically had the highest wages.

Nearly 80 percent of railroad transportation workers are members of unions. Many different railroad unions represent various crafts on the railroads. Most railroad engineers are members of the Brotherhood of Locomotive Engineers, while most other railroad transportation workers are members of the United Transportation Union. Many subway operators are members of the Amalgamated Transit Union, while others belong to the Transport Workers Union of North America.

According to the Bureau of Labor Statistics, jobs in railroad transportation are expected to decrease approximately 18.5 percent between 2000 and 2010.

Sources of Information

More information on salaries, job openings, and job specifications is available from any railroad for which you may want to work or from any of the thirteen unions with which Amtrak has bargaining agreements. You may wish to contact any of the following:

Amtrak
60 Massachusetts Ave. NE
Washington, DC 20002
amtrak.com

Association of American Railroads (AAR)
50 F St. NW
Washington, DC 20001-1564
aar.org

AAR is one of the nation's oldest and most respected trade associations, representing the major freight railroads of the United States, Canada, and Mexico.

Brotherhood of Locomotive Engineers (BLE)
1370 Ontario St., Mezzanine
Cleveland, OH 44113
ble.org

BLE is North America's oldest rail labor union, with more than thirty-five thousand active members in the United States and Canada.

Federal Railroad Administration
400 Seventh St. SW
Washington, DC 20590
fra.dot.gov

United Transportation Union (UTU)
14600 Detroit Ave.
Cleveland, OH 44107-4250
utu.org (United States)
utu-canada.org (Canada)

The UTU is a broad-based transportation labor union representing about 125,000 active and retired railroad, bus, and mass transit workers in the United States and Canada.

Bus Lines

The United States has a magnificent infrastructure to support bus lines: 3,857,356 miles of public roads and streets, including 42,500 miles on the unparalleled interstate highway system.

What a change has taken place since stagecoaches on rudimentary trails were replaced by intercity buses! The first such bus route was established in Oregon, between Bend and Shaniko, in 1905. Early buses, which had solid tires and no springs, were exceedingly uncomfortable and often broke down. Drivers had to be innovative mechanics, but even with the best of efforts, a bus sometimes had to be towed home by a borrowed team of horses.

With today's miles of excellent roads, buses can go almost anywhere in the United States and southern Canada, including large areas not served by airlines or trains. If stronger efforts are made to reduce dependence on private cars, thus helping alleviate both air pollution and fuel expenditure, the use of buses will increase.

The modern intercity bus provides not only transportation, but also large windows and sometimes an upper deck for viewing the scenery. Most also offer air conditioning, rest rooms, and comfortable reclining seats, in addition to a high degree of reliability in meeting schedules and an exceedingly low accident rate. Buses used especially for sightseeing may have tour guides, who point out interesting sights in passing and lead the passengers when they disembark to visit a particular area. Thus, buses are an important and growing segment of the travel scene.

Deregulation of the bus industry in the early 1980s spawned fifteen hundred new bus companies, many of them small but determined to succeed. Greyhound Lines, Inc., the major nationwide intercity bus operator, controls the majority of American buses.

Greyhound Lines is a single corporation. It started in 1914 with a two-mile run for fifteen cents in an open, seven-passenger car, between the Minnesota towns of Hibbing and Alice. In 1987 Greyhound purchased Continental Trailways, its major competitor, and absorbed the Trailways system within its own. Greyhound Lines, Inc., now serves more than twenty-six hundred destinations with eighteen thousand daily departures across the country, and in 2000 it carried more than nineteen million passengers. It currently has approximately five thousand drivers, is based in eighty-eight locations across the country, and employs more than thirteen thousand workers. The company's busiest route is New York to Atlantic City, with well over two thousand passengers traveling between these locations daily. New York to Washington, D.C., is second, with an average of thirteen hundred passengers on the route each day.

Another major bus operator in the travel field is Gray Line Sight-Seeing Companies Associated, Inc., founded in the United States in 1910. This corporation of 150 independently owned long-distance and local sightseeing tour companies is widely recognized and respected as the world's largest sightseeing tour company, serving more than two hundred destinations worldwide. Inquiries about jobs with a Gray Line company can be made to one of its numerous member companies around the world.

Bus drivers held approximately 666,000 jobs in 2000.

Job Responsibilities

Millions of Americans every day leave the driving to bus drivers. Bus drivers are essential in providing passengers with an alternative to their automobiles or other forms of transportation. Motorcoach drivers transport passengers on charter trips and sightseeing tours. Drivers routinely interact with customers and tour guides to make the trip as comfortable and informative as possible. As with all drivers who drive across state or national boundaries, motorcoach drivers must comply with U.S. Department of Transportation regulations. Tour and charter bus drivers may work any day and all hours of the day, including weekends and holidays. Their hours are dictated by the charter trips booked and the schedule and prearranged itinerary of tours. However, like all bus drivers, their weekly hours must be consistent with the Department of Transportation's rules and regulations concerning hours of service. For example, a long-distance driver may not work more than sixty hours in any seven-day period, and drivers must rest eight hours for every ten hours of driving.

Job Requirements

Bus driver qualifications and standards are established by state and federal regulations. All drivers must comply with federal regulations and any state regulations that exceed federal requirements. To qualify for a commercial driver's license, applicants must pass a written test on rules and regulations and then demonstrate they can operate a bus safely. A national data bank permanently records all driving violations incurred by persons who hold commercial licenses. All drivers must be able to read and speak English well enough to read road signs, prepare reports, and communicate with law enforcement officers and the public. In addition, drivers must take a written examination on the Motor Carrier Safety Regulations of the U.S. Department of Transportation.

Many employers prefer high school graduates and require a written test of ability to follow complex bus schedules. Many intercity and public transit bus companies prefer applicants who are at least twenty-four years of age; some require several years of bus or truck driving experience. Because bus drivers deal with passengers, they must be courteous. They need an even temperament and emotional stability, because driving in heavy, fast-moving, or stop-and-go traffic and dealing with passengers can be stressful. Drivers must have very strong customer service abilities, including communication skills and the ability to coordinate and manage large groups of people.

Earnings and Job Outlook

Median hourly earnings of transit and intercity bus drivers were $12.36 in 2000.

The benefits bus drivers receive from their employers vary greatly. Most intercity and local transit bus drivers receive paid health and life insurance, sick leave, and free bus rides on any of the regular routes of their line or system. Drivers who work full-time also get as many as four weeks of vacation annually.

Persons seeking jobs as bus drivers throughout this decade should encounter good opportunities, especially those individuals who have good driving records and who are willing to start with a part-time or irregular schedule.

Local and intercity bus travel is expected to increase as the population and labor force grows. Consequently, employment of local transit and intercity drivers will increase to accommodate the greater number of riders. However, more individual travelers will opt to travel by airplane or automobile rather than by bus. Most growth in intercity drivers will probably be in group charter travel, rather than scheduled intercity bus services.

Most intercity and many local transit bus drivers are members of the Amalgamated Transit Union. Local transit bus drivers in

New York City and several other large cities belong to the Transport Workers Union of America. Some drivers belong to the United Transportation Union and the International Brotherhood of Teamsters.

According to the Bureau of Labor Statistics, jobs for school, transit, and intercity bus drivers are expected to increase by 13.2 percent between 2000 and 2010.

Sources of Information

American Bus Association (ABA)
1100 New York Ave. NW, Ste. 1050
Washington, DC 20005-3934
buses.org

The ABA is the trade association of the intercity bus industry.

American Public Transportation Association (APTA)
1666 K St. NW
Washington, DC 20006
apta.com

APTA members serve the public interest by providing safe, efficient, and economical transit services and by improving those services to meet national energy, environmental, and financial concerns.

Bureau of Labor Statistics
U.S. Department of Labor
2 Massachusetts Ave. NE
Washington, DC 20212-0001
http://stats.bls.gov/oco/ocos242.htm

Canadian Bus Association
451 Daly Ave.
Ottawa, ON
Canada K1N 6H6
buscanada.ca

Gray Line Worldwide
Gray Line House
1835 Gaylord St.
Denver, CO 80206
grayline.com

Greyhound Lines, Inc.
P.O. Box 660362
Dallas, TX 75266-0362
greyhound.com

4

HOTELS, MOTELS, AND RESORTS

THROUGHOUT HISTORY, whenever it was safe to travel, there have been places of public accommodation. In Asia and Asia Minor today, there are small inns called *khans* that provide shelter only. The Bible mentions that the sons of Jacob, returning from Egypt, stopped at such an inn and fed their animals. It was a khan in Bethlehem where Joseph and Mary found no room and had to go to the stables, where Christ was born. Out on the roads, usually at wells, *caravansaries*—huge stone forts large enough to hold one or several caravans with all their animals and strong enough to defend them against attack by bandits—were built at regular intervals. These can still be seen, particularly in Turkey.

Ancient Persians built luxurious inns along their fine road system, as did ancient Romans. When the Romans conquered Britain, they introduced the *taberna* for drinking and the *caupona* for overnight accommodations. During the Dark Ages, travel was possible only by groups that could defend themselves, like small armies. The Knights Hospitallers built many hospices for Crusaders and pilgrims to the Holy Land in the twelfth century, and in western Europe from this time on, abbeys often served as inns—some still do. In England there were about six thousand inns along the high roads and coach routes in the 1500s. Caravansaries had been spaced about eight miles apart, and English inns were fifteen miles apart, showing that a day's journey now covered twice as much distance. The Industrial Revolution spawned railroads, and the resulting increase in travel caused construction of large city hotels. Spa resorts soon followed.

The first known hotel in North America was the Jamestown Inn, built in 1607, the year the colonists arrived in Virginia. A postal service commenced in 1710, after which inns multiplied along the post roads. Resort hotels began opening at eastern U.S. health spas in the 1700s and on the seashore in the 1800s. Large hotels were built around city railroad stations, and as pioneers pushed westward, a hotel was often the first building in a new settlement.

The automobile caused construction of the first "tourist cabins," which later developed into motels. Travel increased with automobiles, and later with aircraft, and hotels proliferated around the world. Several international airlines built hotels in distant, exotic places to provide lodging for their passengers. The industry includes all types of lodging, from upscale hotels to campgrounds, spas, inns, and boardinghouses.

Hotels and motels make up the majority of lodgings. There are also four basic types of hotels—commercial, resort, residential, and extended-stay. The majority of motels and hotels are in the transient or commercial category, and the number of resort hotels is growing rapidly as more people take vacations. About 10 percent of U.S. hotels are residential, meaning that they rent or lease their rooms for long periods to permanent or semipermanent residents.

Extended-stay lodging combines the features of a resort and of a residential hotel. Rooms are much like furnished apartments. For example, they have fully equipped kitchens, computer and telephone hook-ups, and so forth. Usually these rooms are used for a minimum of five consecutive nights.

According to the American Hotel and Lodging Association, in 2000 there were fifty-three thousand properties, 4.1 million rooms, $108.5 billion in sales, and an average occupancy rate of 63.7 percent.

Bricks and mortar provide only part of what the weary traveler wants. Most of the remainder is service, which means people working to fill every request. Out of every dollar taken in by hotels and motels, thirty cents are spent for employees' wages and fringe benefits and the cost of their meals.

Advancement is likely to be faster and further for those who enter the hotel business with an education. There are usually openings at several different entry levels in hotels, with opportunities to advance in various parts of the business.

Many resort hotels used to be open only one season each year. Employees might work in a resort in the Catskill Mountains in New York in summer and in a Florida hotel in winter. Now, however, northern summer hotels are using skiing and other sports to attract a winter clientele, and Florida hotels stay open all year, reducing their rates during the summer.

Many a hotel or motel worker advances by saving money until he or she can set up an independent business. According to the Bureau of Labor Statistics, in 2000 there were approximately sixty-eight thousand hotel managers and assistant managers working for wages or salaries and an additional number of self-employed owners of motels and small hotels.

Job Responsibilities

Modern hotels offer much more than rooms and meals for travelers. The variety of services they provide adds to the number and types of hotel jobs. Besides guest rooms and restaurants, a hotel may have special bars or nightclubs; banquet facilities; meeting rooms with audiovisual and translation equipment; large ballrooms; sales exhibit rooms; swimming pools; marinas, golf courses, or tennis courts; ski tows and lifts; travel agencies; beauty and barber shops; valet services; airline offices; theater ticket agencies; newsstands; gift shops; baby-sitting services; car, boat, and plane rentals; health clubs; stage and film theaters; and gambling casinos. Today, many hotels offer cutting-edge technology to accomplish state-of-the-art meetings and conventions. They have on-site information technology staff, any number of means to connect to the Internet, and videoconferencing capabilities.

A large hotel may have six major departments and some auxiliary ones. The executive department may include a general manager, resident manager, controllers or accountants, management trainees, and directors of sales, personnel, rooms, food and beverages, housekeeping, and public relations.

In the front office are people directly responsible for personal contact with the guests. These include mail clerks, room clerks, reservation clerks, and the front-office manager. The accounting department has auditors, bookkeepers, office-machine operators, cashiers, and other clerical workers responsible for handling the operation of the business.

The housekeeping department includes the housekeeper, housekeeper's assistants, heavy-cleaning people, seamstresses, tailors, launderers, decorators, upholsterers, and others. Redcaps, valets, elevator operators, and door people work under the superintendent of service in the service department. They are responsible for maintaining a neat and clean home for visitors.

The restaurant department has chefs, cooks of various grades and types, kitchen helpers, a steward and staff, pantry keepers, storeroom employees, dishwashers, food servers, bartenders, bus people, and other food and beverage service workers.

The maintenance department has stationary engineers to operate machinery for heating and air-conditioning guest rooms and public rooms, and for cooling large refrigerators. This department also employs electricians, plumbers, carpenters, painters, and locksmiths.

Front-Office Workers

Front-office clerks do much of the hotel's minute-by-minute business with guests. The room clerks rent rooms and greet guests, assign rooms, sell various services, open billing records for new guests, advise housekeepers of arrivals and departures, and keep reservations lists. When a room is assigned, the desk clerk turns the key over to a bell person who takes the guest to the room.

Reservation clerks receive reservations in person or by mail, fax, telephone, or Internet, and acknowledge them. They type out registration forms and advise room clerks of each day's list of arriving guests. Reservations for hotel and motel rooms are now mostly done over the Internet so that a traveler has instant confirmation of a reservation.

Mail and information clerks place mail, messages, and keys in guests' boxes and give these out when called for. They answer telephones and route incoming calls to the right rooms. They also may sell stamps and advise guests about transportation, attractions, and events.

Most of North America's elegant hotels now have a concierge sitting at a prominent desk in the lobby. This is often a personable young woman or man who speaks several languages. The functions of the concierge are many and varied. He or she provides guests with all sorts of information; arranges reservations or tickets for dinner, the theater, airlines, tours, sports facilities, or events; arranges introductions; lends umbrellas when it rains; and solves any guest room problems of heat, cold, humidity, plumbing, or other inconvenience. The symbol of the concierge is crossed keys on the lapels. The position and the term *concierge*, long common in Europe, became widespread in North American luxury hotels in the 1980s.

The front-office manager supervises all these functions, coordinates the actions of the front office with those of the housekeeper and others, schedules work shifts and assignments of clerks, inspects rooms periodically, and handles the many kinds of complaints and problems that can arise in a hotel. Most front offices never close, so if clerks fail to arrive, the manager must find substitutes or fill in for the absent clerk.

Cashiers keep track of guest charges, total them when a guest leaves or at regular intervals, and accept payment. Accountants bill guests regularly, handle the hotel's payroll, and prepare regular profit-and-loss statements.

For the person who is ambitious for success in the hotel business, the front office is the place to learn all about hotels and how to cope with all the problems that can arise. Inexperienced newcomers usually fill openings for beginners' clerical jobs in the front office. Sometimes bell people, switchboard operators, or other employees who appear capable are promoted to such jobs.

Education and Training

Educational requirements for front-office jobs vary according to the type and size of hotel, its location, and its own standards. A high school education is desirable. Graduates of two- or four-year colleges often start as management trainees, rotating from one department to another, but obtaining major experience in the front office. Even better for such a career is graduation from a two- or four-year course in hotel and motel management. These specialized curricula are becoming widespread as colleges realize the growing importance of the lodging industry. (See the Appendix for a list of U.S. schools.)

It is still possible for a person without a high school education, but with a good personality and native ability and intelligence, to rise to the top in the lodging business. Such advancement becomes more difficult, however, as college-trained people enter the business as management trainees. So it makes sense to obtain the best education you can. In addition to more rapid advancement, the person with greater education is generally paid more in top management positions.

If you want to enter the lodging business directly after high school, try to attend a technical high school offering hotel-related courses. Courses that might be beneficial include cooking, business administration, management, and economics.

For its employees who have little or no education, the hotel industry provides training courses. In New York City, for example, the Hotel Association, in cooperation with the Hotel and Motel Trades Council, AFL-CIO, operates its Industry Training Program. Free fifteen-week courses that combine classroom and on-the-job training are given at various hours to accommodate people on different shifts. Courses include English, basic accounting, repairs and maintenance, food and beverage control, floor housekeeping, telephone switchboard operation, night auditing, business machine operation, typing, and front-office procedures. There are similar programs in many cities. Many hotel workers who started as maids or busboys have profited by these courses to become housekeepers, cashiers, auditors, and room clerks among other higher-level jobs.

High schools in many cities have adult education programs with specific courses for hotel workers. Some large hotels and chains have their own in-house schools, combining formal classes with on-the-job training.

An industry educational program applicable to a variety of situations is that of the Educational Institute of the American Hotel and Lodging Association (AH&LA-EI). (See the Sources of Information section at the end of this chapter for contact information.) These courses can be taken by mail on an individual basis, in small groups without an instructor, in larger groups with instructors, or through cooperating colleges that teach institute courses, as well as online courses. Courses cover many topics, from the basics of sanitation and bookkeeping on up to marketing and hotel/motel property management. People can take single courses in a special-interest subject, such as food and beverage operations, or take ten courses and earn the Institute's diploma. Beyond this, by taking five courses in advanced management, having five years of industry experience, and demonstrating service to the industry, a hotel worker can earn distinction as a certified hotel administrator.

Earnings and Job Outlook

Employment at hotels, motels, and resorts has advantages and disadvantages. There is always room for advancement for the hard worker who is willing to study and learn. Work in the lodging industry offers variety. When a person reaches the top in a small operation, he or she can generally move to a larger one and keep advancing. A person with a good record can usually find work in any part of the traveled world, and certainly in any part of the United States or Canada. Hotel workers in a chain usually can vacation in the chain's various properties at a fraction of the regular fee.

Bus person and housekeeper wages are low, but job security is good and meals and uniforms are often provided, so that the cost of living is reduced.

At the middle-management level, salaries are good compared to those in other industries, and at top management levels, the salaries can be very high. Hours worked per week are comparable with those in other industries, but many jobs must be performed at night, on Sundays, and on holidays, which can disrupt social or family life.

The following table from the Bureau of Labor Statistics shows the median hourly earnings in the year 2000 of the largest occupations in hotels and other lodging places.

Occupations	*Hotels/Motels*
Lodging managers	$14.95
Maintenance and repair workers, general	9.98
Cooks, restaurant	9.96
Security guards	9.61
Hotel, motel, and resort desk clerks	7.84
Laundry and dry-cleaning workers	7.48
Maids and housekeeping cleaners	7.09
Baggage porters and bellhops	6.74
Waiters and waitresses	6.60
Gaming dealers	6.26

The Bureau of Labor Statistics predicts that wage and salary employment in hotels and other lodging places will increase 13 percent between 2000 and 2010, slower than the 16-percent growth projected for all industries combined. This growth reflects rising personal income, an increase in the number of two-income families, low-cost airfares, emphasis on leisure activities, and growth of foreign tourism in the United States. In addition, special packages for short vacations and weekend travel should stimulate employment growth. As more states legalize some form of gambling, the hotel industry will invest in gaming.

Job opportunities should be concentrated in the largest hotel occupations, such as building cleaning workers and hotel, motel, and resort desk clerks. Many of these openings will be in resorts, spas, and full-service hotels.

Employment outlook varies by occupation. Employment of hotel, motel, and resort desk clerks is expected to grow rapidly as some of these move up to managerial positions. However, the spread of computer technology will cause employment of other clerical workers, such as bookkeepers, accountants, and auditing clerks and secretaries, to grow more slowly than the industry as a whole. Employment of waiters and waitresses will no doubt decline since the trend is for hotels and other lodging places not to offer full-service restaurants.

The employment of lodging managers is expected to increase more slowly than that within the overall hotel industry since the economy-class establishments will have fewer departments to manage. However, the trend toward chain-affiliated lodging places should provide managers with opportunities for advancement into general manager positions and corporate administrative jobs. Jobs for lodging managers are expected to increase by 9.3 percent between 2000 and 2010.

Job turnover is high in this industry. To attract and retain workers, the lodging industry is placing more emphasis on hiring and training.

Sources of Information

For information on various careers in hotels, motels, and resorts, contact the following:

Hospitality Careers

American Hotel and Lodging Association (AH&LA)
1201 New York Ave. NW, Ste. 600
Washington, DC 20005-3931
ahlaonline.org

AH&LA is a ninety-two-year-old federation of state lodging associations throughout the United States with some thirteen thousand property members worldwide, representing more than 1.7 million guest rooms. Its website has links to hospitality schools, hospitality-related associations, lodging industry trade press, and state hotel and lodging associations.

American Hotel and Lodging Educational Foundation (AH&LEF)
1201 New York Ave. NW, Ste. 600
Washington, DC 20005-3931
ahlf.org

AH&LEF provides financial support that enhances the stability, prosperity, and growth of the lodging industry through educational and research programs.

Educational Institute of the American Hotel and Lodging
   Association (AH&LA-EI)
800 N. Magnolia Ave., Ste. 1800
Orlando, FL 32803
ei-ahma.org

AH&LA-EI is the premier source for providing industry-tested,
research-driven, hospitality training resources worldwide.

International Council on Hotel, Restaurant, and Institutional
   Education (I-CHRIE)
3205 Skipwith Rd.
Richmond, VA 23294-4442
chrie.org

I-CHRIE is the global advocate of hospitality and tourism education
for schools, colleges, and universities offering programs in hotel and
restaurant management, food-service management, and culinary arts.

Food and Beverage Service

American Culinary Federation, Inc. (ACF)
10 San Bartola Dr.
St. Augustine, FL 32086
acfchefs.org

ACF is a professional, not-for-profit organization for chefs and cooks.
Its goal is to promote the professional image of American chefs worldwide through education among culinarians at all levels, from appren-
tices to the most accomplished certified master chefs. Contact the
ACF for information about apprenticeship and certification programs
for cooks.

National Restaurant Association
1200 Seventeenth St. NW
Washington, DC 20036-3097
restaurant.org

The National Restaurant Association is the leading business association for the restaurant industry. Together with the National Restaurant Association Educational Foundation, the association's mission is to represent, educate, and promote a rapidly growing industry that is comprised of 858,000 restaurant and food-service outlets employing 11.3 million people.

Housekeeping and Janitorial

Service Employees International Union (SEIU)
1313 L St. NW
Washington, DC 20005
seiu.org

The Service Employees International Union is made up of 1.5 million working service employees and 120,000 retirees united to improve their jobs and communities.

Housekeeping Management

International Executive Housekeepers Association (IEHA)
1001 Eastwind Dr., Ste. 301
Westerville, OH 43081
ieha.org

The IEHA is a professional and educational organization of approximately six thousand members involved in or directly affiliated with the various facilities management and allied professions.

5

TRAVEL AGENCIES

TODAY TRAVEL AGENCIES are deeply concerned that their customers will start dealing directly with hotels and carriers via the Internet, bypassing the agencies. Thirty-nine percent of travelers who go online think the Internet is easier and faster to use for travel planning than is a travel agent, according to the "Yesawich, Pepperdine, & Brown and Yankelovich Partners' 2002 National Travel Monitor" report. In addition, the expansion of electronic ticketing—not to mention airlines cutting back on agency commissions, passenger fear of air travel, and the economic situation—make travel agent employment a slow-growth travel occupation.

However, many consumers still find the process of booking a vacation on their own cumbersome and time-consuming and prefer to hire a professional travel agent to ensure a good holiday at a good price. The 2002 National Travel Monitor also states that although use of the Internet for researching and booking travel arrangements is higher than in previous years, three out of every ten leisure travelers still use the services of a travel agent. Travel agents' responsibilities are concerned more with adding value to leisure or corporate travel itineraries rather than actually booking the trip.

According to the Bureau of Labor Statistics, travel agents in 2000 held 135,000 jobs, and more than eight out of ten salaried agents worked for travel agencies. The remainder worked for other travel organizations.

History

Ticket agencies have existed since ancient Rome, when postal employees sold tickets for the use of chariots and roads and made out an *itinerarium*—the ancestor of the modern traveler's itinerary. Operators of packet boats, stagecoaches, trams, railways, and steamships sold tickets in their offices for rides on their equipment.

Thomas Cook, a printer in England, started the business of the general travel agency; that is, the selling of tickets and tours that utilized the facilities of other companies. Railroads had just commenced operation, and Cook, an ardent nondrinker, wanted to use them to advance the temperance cause. In 1844, he chartered a train to carry people from Loughborough to Leicester, where they would attend a temperance convention and return. Charging twenty-five cents each, he crowded 541 people aboard this first special train—the first round-trip ticket in history.

Cook operated other temperance tours that were very popular. He soon realized that people were more attracted by travel at low prices than by temperance, so he began operating tours for entertainment, education, and other purposes. Ten years after his first tour, 165,000 people used his transportation and lodging arrangements to visit a great fair at the Crystal Palace in London. Cook opened a London office in 1865, by which time he was already sending tours to Europe and the Holy Land. In 1866 he led the first escorted American pleasure tour, visiting cities such as New York; Washington, D.C.; Richmond; Cincinnati; Toronto; and Montreal; and sites including Civil War battlefields, Mammoth Cave, and Niagara Falls. In 1872 he led a tour of twenty-two people around the world. His son John M. Cook promoted the firm in America and other places outside Britain. In 1874, Cook introduced what were called *circular notes*. In a slightly different form, these became known as traveler's checks, which today are issued by Cook's, American Express, and several of the major North American and European banks.

American Express, another major travel agency, was established in 1850 with the merger of the firms of Henry Wells and William G. Fargo, who also organized Wells Fargo two years later. Initially American Express was a shipping concern, but it moved into banking and tourist services and by 1918 was out of the freight business.

Cook's, American Express, and a number of other large agencies organize and operate their own tours, as well as sell tickets for all kinds of travel. They also make individual travel arrangements, and some agencies specialize in certain national destinations to which they send frequent charter tours. Others arrange trips for youth groups, ski enthusiasts, and other particular interest groups.

Today

Most travel agencies do not organize tours themselves. Instead, they are in the business of selling trips and tours that are offered by travel wholesalers and carriers. As of June 2002, the American Society of Travel Agents (ASTA) estimated there are about twenty-seven thousand travel agency locations (including branches) in the

United States. Some of these are operated solely by the owner; however, the average agency has five or six full-time and one or two part-time employees.

Travel agents give out a tremendous amount of advice and information to prospective travelers, but they make no money unless they sell tickets and hotel reservations. Working for a travel agency, therefore, means selling; so a person not interested in selling should not enter the agency business. There are benefits to the travel agent's job—like free or inexpensive "familiarization" trips by carriers and hotels—but the new employee is not likely to receive these. Low-cost air travel and hotel rooms are usually made available after a probationary period, but for the first few years, an agency employee might be able to use these only on her or his annual one- or two-week vacation.

Travel-agency employees need to be able to find specific information rapidly on all kinds of schedules, fares, special excursions, tour offerings, car rentals, guide services, seasonally varying hotel rates, and a host of other details. It usually takes many months for a new employee to become really useful in an agency, especially a small agency. In a vast concern like American Express, jobs are compartmentalized and easier to learn.

Job Responsibilities

An employee of a travel agency takes on quite a variety of tasks. She or he gives out travel literature about destinations; airline and cruise "packages" that cover almost all costs for transportation, accommodations, and meals; bus tours in the local area; and perhaps helicopter and train tours. The agent answers questions about comparative costs for accommodations and transportation as prospective travelers seek the least expensive or most luxurious vacations. She or he makes out itineraries that can be quite long and complicated if there are numerous stops and various hotels. When the client has approved a proposed itinerary, the agency clerk has to issue tickets and vouchers, sending copies to airlines and hotels to confirm reservations made by telephone, fax, mail, or E-mail.

Travel agency personnel sell travelers' checks and special tickets such as Eurail passes; they also arrange for rental cars and escorted tours. By agreement with other travel agencies around the world, they can offer all kinds of local services in any city the traveler might reach.

Business in a travel agency changes from month to month, according to current attractions and time and money available to travelers. School and business vacations determine when many people take trips. The rich and the retired go south in winter and the energetic go skiing. Resort areas have high seasons and low seasons, and they are always trying to extend the high season a little longer with special attractions. For example, Atlantic City's Miss America contest was designed to add a week to the short summer season, and it has been successful at this for eight decades. Many places have notable annual events, such as Carneval in Rio de Janeiro, Mardi Gras in New Orleans, New Year's Eve in New York's Times Square, and Oktoberfest in Bavaria. For major world events such as the Olympic Games and for popular cruises, accommodations are booked well in advance.

Requests to an agency are changing constantly, and clerks must remain alert to new tours, excursions, special fare offerings, and constantly changing fares and schedules.

A large part of the agent's business is arranging travel and accommodations for business travelers. This, in fact, constituted the greater part of the travel business until the 1970s, when tourism became larger in gross billings than business travel. Some large corporations have their own in-house travel personnel to make direct bookings with carriers.

Requirements

Qualification to work in a travel agency varies widely from one office to another, and some agencies will accept people with less than a high school education. All, however, prefer applicants who have completed high school. College training, of course, enables one to move up faster and further. Beginners often start as administrative assistants. As they do the paperwork, they gradually learn about the business and can begin to answer inquiries and deal with the public.

For the student who hopes to enter a travel agency upon graduation from high school, valuable experience can be accumulated as a part-time employee working one or two hours per day on Saturdays or during summer vacations.

There is no federal licensing requirement for a travel agent. However, fourteen states have regulations that stipulate travel agents must have a license to sell certain travel products. The website for the American Society of Travel Agents lists these states. For further information, contact your state's Office of the Attorney General or Department of Commerce.

Education and Training

Vocational schools offer six- to twelve-week travel agent programs. Travel agent courses are offered in community colleges, four-year colleges, and adult education centers. In addition, there are bachelor's or master's degrees in travel and tourism. A list of U.S. schools by state can be found on the ASTA website.

For entry-level travel agents, the Institute of Certified Travel Agents (ICTA) offers excellent books on a travel agent career, including the nation's leading travel and tourism textbook, *Travel Career Development*, 7th edition. This book is an authoritative, single-source text that provides the educational foundation students will need in the travel industry. (See the Sources of Information section at the end of this chapter for a list of books.)

The national TAP Test is a basic competency test that measures the entry-level knowledge of travel professionals within all aspects of the travel industry. ICTA, ASTA, and other industry partners developed the test to provide a national standard of excellence for the travel industry. The test is given on scheduled or open dates in selected cities in the United States.

The Certified Travel Associate (CTA) program is ICTA's first level of certification and was introduced in 1997 to meet the needs of travel professionals in the early stages of their careers. The CTA program focuses on the knowledge and the sales skills necessary for effective practice in the travel industry. It covers four core skill areas: communication and technology, geography, sales and service, and the travel business itself. CTAs must possess eighteen months of full-time industry experience and are required to earn ten continuing education units each year to maintain their designation. The CTA program represents 40 percent of the study necessary for the CTC program, and many CTAs go on to achieve their CTC designations.

The Certified Travel Counselor (CTC) designation is the pinnacle of travel industry professionalism. The CTC curriculum covers three core skill areas: business development, contemporary issues, and professional development. CTC candidates are required to complete twelve courses in which they learn how to negotiate effectively, make dynamic presentations, analyze new business opportunities, implement technological solutions, plan for the future, and more. The first level of ICTA certification, the CTA, must be successfully completed in order to earn the CTC designation. CTCs must possess at least five years of full-time travel industry experience and are required to earn ten continuing education credits each year to maintain their designation.

For the new employee in a travel agency, there are courses that help her or him learn the business much faster than would be possible by accumulated experience alone. ASTA provides five home study or online specialist courses, the cost of which is reduced if the student is a member of or employed by a member of ASTA. Costs cover instruction material, exams, evaluation, and E-mail support. The course titles are Family Travel Specialist, Niche Travel Specialist, Mature Adult Travel Specialist, North American Rail Travel Specialist, and Travel Marketing Specialist.

One way to earn continuing education credits each year is to take one of ICTA's thirteen Destination Specialist (DS) courses. The Destination Specialist courses provide travel industry professionals with detailed knowledge of specific world areas, enabling them to match clients with the right travel products. Each course features destination highlights, sample itineraries, and cultural insights. The thirteen programs cover Africa, Alaska, the Caribbean, China, East Asia, Eastern Europe, European culture and heritage, Hawaii, Latin America, North America, the South Pacific, special-interest travel, and Western Europe. Each DS course includes a comprehensive textbook with extensive maps, a world atlas, a practical study guide, and a job aid. Upon successful completion, ICTA will provide a diploma that states a country of specialization.

ICTA offers educational workshops and featured speakers live via its online E-Learning Center. You can go online to view speakers discuss topics such as CTA Preparation or the Seven Habits of Highly Effective Travel Agents. Costs for these sessions are reduced for ICTA members.

ASTA Foundation, Inc., is a nonprofit subsidiary of the American Society of Travel Agents. The foundation offers more than twenty scholarships for the most qualified students in a bachelor's, master's, doctoral, community college, or travel school program, and to travel professionals seeking to further their education.

The Cruise Lines International Association (CLIA), headquartered in New York, represents nearly 95 percent of the North American cruise industry. In 1993 CLIA introduced a major Cruise Counselor Certification Program, which provides travel agents with advanced courses that lead to an Accredited Cruise Counselor (ACC) or Master Cruise Counselor (MCC) designation. Credits are earned via a combination of classroom training, video training, Internet training, cruise experience, attendance at CLIA cosponsored conferences, ship inspections, CLIA Institute participation, completion of CLIA's new textbook, and case studies. Credit is also given for completion of CTA and CTC designations mentioned in preceding paragraphs.

Employment

How does one get a job in a travel agency? Jobs in online or in classified advertisement sections of newspapers generally are listed under the "Travel" heading. Most such advertisements demand experience in an agency or in similar work for an airline or other carrier or hotel. A newcomer in the field should search online or look for ads for "travel trainees," "travel entry level" positions, or for clerical, typists, assistants, or even messengers—anything to get inside an agency so you can start accumulating the necessary experience that helps qualify you for a better agency job. ASTA's website has a job bank that lets you select on the basis of job functions and location.

The trade press of the travel industry also carries advertisements for positions. Among the publications you should check for help-wanted ads are *Travel Agent Magazine*, *Travel Weekly*, and *TravelAge West*. (See the Sources of Information section at the end of this chapter for websites.) These publications circulate only to travel agencies, but an agency will probably give you a few copies if you ask.

You can approach very large travel agencies directly any time because they must frequently hire trainees to replace other employees who have been promoted or moved. Corporate mergers of giant companies have occurred in the travel field as well as in most other industries. American Express purchased Thomas Cook Travel and is now called American Express Travel Related Services, Inc. Carlson Travel Network merged with Wagon Lits Travel and is now called Carlson Wagonlit Travel. IVI Travel merged with U.S. Travel System and is now called WorldTravel BTI. These and Rosenbluth Travel are the top companies in business and corporate travel. Each of these companies has sales in the billions of dollars every year.

An agency usually rents or buys one of the global distribution systems (GDS), which are computer reservations systems used by the industry. The major GDSs used in the United States today are

Sabre, Amadeus, Worldspan, and Galileo. A large agency might join two systems to avoid the "reservation bias" that can be built into any single system. Familiarity with at least one of these systems, plus knowledge of personal computers and their operating systems, can increase your salary by thousands of dollars in a travel agency; by the same token, computer illiteracy can stop you dead.

Travel positions are handled by personnel agencies, and there are a few travel-job specialists. Yours in Travel Personnel Agency, Inc. (aka Yours in Travel Group) was founded by P. Jason King in New York in 1972. Today, with branch locations in more than ten cities, Yours in Travel is the nation's largest recruitment source for the travel, tourism, transportation, and hospitality industries. The company is also global, servicing four continents. Yours in Travel recruits personnel for many companies in the travel and tourism industries throughout North America and overseas. Salaries range from $20,000 for travel school graduates and for well-traveled beginners up to $500,000 for senior executives.

Earnings and Job Outlook

According to a 2000 survey conducted by *Travel Counselor Magazine*, the median annual salary for a travel agent was $31,500, up 5 percent from 1999. Eight percent took home $60,000 or more, and 17 percent earned less than $18,000. The size and type (leisure versus business) of the travel agency, experience of the agent, and the location all are determining factors of salaries.

Airline commissions—for both domestic and international tickets—make up a large portion of travel agency commissions. A big debate occurring now centers around commissions airlines pay to travel agents: in March 2002 the major airlines started the final round to reduce base commissions to zero, and some airlines continue to have performance-based programs that pay override commissions. Car rental companies following in the footsteps of the airlines are eliminating agents' commissions for corporate rentals.

Commissions for travel arrangements, cruises, hotels, and sightseeing tours run about 7 to 10 percent of the total sale. Rail commissions run about 5 percent of the total sale. Approximately 29 percent of travel agents receive compensation by salary alone, 15 percent are paid commission only, and 56 percent receive a combination of salary and commission and/or bonuses.

Travel agents more and more are charging fees for such noncommissionable services as obtaining visas for a traveler, sending faxes, making long-distance telephone calls for last-minute reservations, and working out especially complicated itineraries. If a carefully planned trip is canceled, an agent is likely to charge a planning fee.

A special type of travel wholesaler is the tour consolidator, who arranges the cheapest form of air travel—charter trips. There are usually no hotel or dining arrangements with such trips—only round-trip air transportation. The consolidator charters an airplane, or perhaps a block of seats, and sells transportation through advertisements or, more typically, to clubs or occupational groups that take care of the clerical work and collect the money for the trip. The work of the consolidator requires knowledge of airlines, a willingness to take risks, selling ability, and usually a fairly large amount of capital. One way to acquire the necessary skills is to work for a consolidator or in the charter department of an airline.

Just as in any other job, there are certain disadvantages associated with working for a travel agency or being a travel agent. The business is seasonal, making it necessary for some employees to be laid off for a part of every year. Most people consider pleasure travel a luxury; therefore, it is often one of the first things to be cut from the family budget when there is an economic downturn. Agents can cope with a minor economic downturn by scheduling clients for relatively inexpensive forms of travel, but in a very serious recession, travel agencies may be forced out of business.

For employees just starting in the travel agency business, there is a great deal of detail work, which some people do not enjoy. Travel agents also deal with the public constantly, and a few travelers—the haughty, supercilious, and demanding—are very hard to please. At peak seasons, a travel agent often must work long hours with constant interruptions by clients.

Despite the best efforts of travel agents, travel arrangements can be upset by such unexpected distant events as a strike of airline flight attendants in Iceland or of airline mechanics in Paris, or an earthquake in Nicaragua or Greece. The agent then must work frantically to save as much as possible of an itinerary and re-plan the rest.

Because of the allure of travel, many young people are attracted to jobs in travel agencies. By the law of supply and demand, large supply means low price; therefore, beginning personnel are not well paid. For this reason, personal travel is considered to be part of a travel agency employee's pay.

Examine your reasons for wanting to be a travel agency employee or owner. If the main attraction is personal travel, you may want to rethink the matter thoroughly. Could you earn higher pay in another industry and perhaps travel just as much? You would be paying for your travel, of course, but as a paid passenger, you would experience no waiting for hours for space-available seats, nor would you be bumped at the last minute just because one more ticket-holding passenger came aboard.

On the other hand, people who stick with an agency can advance to earning generous salaries, having time off when they want it, and getting the pick of their travel desires over most of the world. A travel agent can sometimes please clients best by pleasing herself or himself. F. C. M. Pauwels, a travel agent who operated the five-person Plaza Travel Service in New York, liked music and the Orient. So as part of his regular work, he led groups of music lovers on three- or four-week tours of European music festivals and others on tours of the Orient.

According to the Bureau of Labor Statistics, jobs for travel agents are expected to increase by 3.2 percent between 2000 and 2010.

Self-Employment

Should you go into the travel-agency business yourself—as owner, owner-manager, or partner? If you have the capital it is not difficult, because agencies are always for sale as owners retire or decide to sell for other reasons. If you are not experienced in the travel-agency field, it would be much better to buy a partnership in a going business rather than buy a business outright and try to operate it from scratch.

What about the possibility of simply renting a store and putting up a sign to say that you're a travel agent? This probably would not work at all, since you would not be accredited to sell the tickets of the major carriers, and, therefore, would have to buy tickets through another agent and split the commissions.

A growing number of professional travel agents choose to work from home, either as outside sales employees or independent contractors. Outside sales are compensated by commissions and independent contractors keep all the commission earned from sales, but they pay a fee to a travel agency that issues the tickets or provides them services. In both scenarios, when they build up enough capital, know-how, and familiarity with the accrediting agencies, they go into business for themselves. Other people have done the same sort of thing, starting by chartering buses for church and club outings and selling tickets—just as Thomas Cook did at the beginning of his business—and gradually working up to becoming travel wholesalers. The National Association of Commissioned Travel Agents, Inc. (NACTA) is the travel industry's leading association for independent travel agents, cruise-oriented agents, home-based travel agents, and outside-sales travel agents. Books on becoming a home-based travel agent can be researched on the Internet using keywords such as "home based travel agent" or "spare time travel agent."

To be an agent of any kind, you have to represent one or more principals. A principal can be an airline, cruise line, or a purveyor of lodging, food, and other services. An agent can be appointed directly by a supplier, as is typical with hotels, car rental companies, and tour operators. The other way is to be appointed by a coordinating body accepted by various suppliers. The two coordinating bodies for the airlines are the Airlines Reporting Cooperation (ARC) and the International Airlines Travel Agency Network (IATAN). When an established agency is sold, the new owner must qualify for her or his appointments. For cruise lines, the coordinating body is the Cruise Line International Association (CLIA), and for trains it is Amtrak.

Sources of Information

Information on various travel agent–related organizations can be found by contacting the following:

Travel Agent Associations

American Society of Travel Agents (ASTA)
1101 King St., Ste. 200
Alexandria, VA 22314
asta.org

ASTA, primarily an association of travel agencies, is the major trade association for travel agents.

Association of Canadian Travel Agents
130 Albert St., Ste. 1705
Ottawa, ON
Canada K1P 5G4
acta.ca

ACTA is a national trade association representing the retail travel sector of Canada's tourism industry.

Institute of Certified Travel Agents (ICTA)
148 Linden St.
Wellesley, MA 02181
icta.com

ICTA is an international, nonprofit organization that educates and certifies travel industry professionals at all career stages.

Books available from ICTA include:

Travel Career Development, 7th edition

Travel Career Development, 7th edition, Student Workbook

Travel Career Development, 7th edition, Instructor's
   Resource Manual

Travel Sales and Customer Service, 2nd edition
Travel Sales and Customer Service Instructor's Resource Manual, 2nd edition
Exploring the World: Geography for Travel Professionals

Other Travel Organizations

Airlines Reporting Corporation (ARC)
4100 N. Fairfax Dr., Ste. 600
Arlington, VA 22203-1629
arccorp.com

The purpose of ARC is to be the preferred provider of services related primarily to distribution and settlement of travel purchased in the United States on behalf of ARC's owner airlines, participating carriers, authorized travel agencies, and customers.

Amtrak
National Railroad Passenger Corporation
60 Massachusetts Ave. NE, 4th Fl.
Washington, DC 20002-4285
amtrak.com

(For more on railroads, see Chapter 3.)

Cruise Lines International Association
500 Fifth Ave., Ste. 1407
New York, NY 10110
cruising.org

(For more on cruise lines, see Chapter 3.)

International Airlines Travel Agency Network (IATAN)
300 Garden City Plaza, Ste. 342
Garden City, NY 11530-3302
iatan.org

IATAN provides a vital link between the supplier community and the U.S. travel distribution network.

National Association of Commissioned Travel Agents, Inc.
   (NACTA)
1101 King St., Ste. 300
Alexandria, VA 22314
nacta.com

NACTA is the travel industry's leading association for independent travel agents, cruise-oriented agents, home-based travel agents, and outside-sales travel agents.

Travel Industry Association (TIA)
1100 New York Ave. NW, Ste. 450
Washington, DC 20005-3934
tia.org

TIA is a nonprofit association that represents and speaks for the common interests and concerns of all components of the U.S. travel industry.

United States Tour Operators Association (USTOA)
275 Madison Ave., Ste. 2014
New York, NY 10016
ustoa.com

The USTOA is a professional association representing the tour operator industry.

Trade Publications

TravelAge West: travelagewest.com
Travel Agent Magazine: travelagentcentral.com
Travel Trade: traveltrade.com
Travel Weekly: travelweekly.com

6

PUBLIC RELATIONS

THE TRAVEL INDUSTRY must rely heavily on advertising and promotion to attract the crowds of travelers on whom it depends. Advertising, on the scale required to promote a Caribbean island, for example, is very expensive. When funds are scarce for advertising, the ingenious public relations professional fills the void by obtaining publicity through visits by travel writers and travel agents and celebrities, through celebrations and fairs and local events that merit press notice, and through all manner of innovative activities that legitimately draw attention. Even with a generous advertising budget, all these activities remain important in continuing to attract travelers.

Persuasion through communication is the job of the public relations professional. More specifically, public relations for travel concerns the relations of corporations, governments, hotels, carriers, resorts, cities, and other organizations with their own employees, business travelers, pleasure travelers, and the public at large. Among the media used by public relations experts to influence people are newspapers, magazines, books, radio, television, speeches, photographs, advertisements, surveys, exhibitions, charts, receptions, and parties. Workers in public relations may serve inside the organization being publicized, or they may belong to an outside company specializing in public relations for one or many organizations.

In 2000, public relations managers held approximately 74,000 jobs, according to the Bureau of Labor Statistics. There were approximately 707,000 advertising, marketing, promotions, public relations, and sales managers working in all industries in 2000.

History

From the most ancient times, rulers paid writers and songsmiths to create works that praised the ruler, inspired patriotism, and persuaded people of the worthiness of the current war.

These were direct, naive public relations efforts, and there are thousands of similar examples throughout history. But the term *public relations* did not come into use until early in this century. Before that, the Roman Catholic Church had instituted the word *propaganda* to describe its efforts to mold public opinion in the Counter-Reformation, and press agents were employed by both the North and the South in the Civil War to influence European public opinion. *Propaganda* eventually became a dirty word because people realized that much of it was false. Similarly, the term *press agent* is seldom used now because of the work of press agents in covering up or glorifying nefarious schemes of the robber barons of American industry in the late 1800s. The ridiculously excessive publicity stunts of press agents for Hollywood stars and other celebrities also added to their tainted image.

Public relations in its modern context started largely with Ivy L. Lee and Edward L. Betrays. Lee, hired in 1906 as publicity adviser to the Pennsylvania Railroad, began a policy of openness and frankness with reporters. For example, instead of trying to suppress press awareness of a terrible train wreck, he invited reporters to the scene and helped them to determine and report the cause of the accident.

Rather than just accepting orders to flaunt good news or suppress bad news, Lee and Betrays both gave advice to their clients. Betrays studied the people he was trying to influence and decided there were several different "publics" to be reached, and each had to be approached in the most effective way.

In 1927, John W. Hill, a newspaperman, opened a one-man public relations company in Cleveland. His firm, Hill and Knowlton, became the largest public relations firm in the world, with offices in New York and seven other U.S. cities, as well as in ten European and Asian cities. Mr. Hill, who died in 1977, once said:

> Since the aim of public relations is to inform and convince, the good public relations person has a talent both for understanding and for telling. He enjoys explaining things to others and, like a good debater, wants to persuade. The public relations person thus tends to have an aptitude for expression. He is likely to be a good writer or speaker. Choosing the right word at the right time is of real importance to him, for he is sensitive to people's responses. The good public relations person has curiosity and thoroughness, too. To convince others, he must himself know; and to know, he has to dig. Thus the good public relations person has factual knowledge, but knows people, too—how and why they react, when and how to present his message. He must be concerned equally with the big problem and the small detail.

David Ogilvy, an advertising genius, emphasized the value of public relations in promoting tourism:

> Give your public relations budget priority over your advertising budget. . . . There is almost no limit to the amount of free publicity a country can get in newspapers, magazines, television and radio provided you don't starve your public relations people. . . . If I were running a national tourism office in the United States, I wouldn't spend a penny on advertising until I had spent $250,000 on public relations.

And as the Public Relations Society points out:

> Public relations, at its best, does not only tell an organization's "story" to its publics. The public relations practitioner also helps shape his organization and the way it performs.

Job Responsibilities

There can be a great deal of variety in public relations work. The functions of the public relations agency or division can be broken down into eight specific kinds of work:

1. Conducting research and evaluation
2. Defining goals and planning public relations campaigns
3. Building working relationships
4. Writing and editing
5. Disseminating information
6. Producing communications
7. Developing special events
8. Speaking publicly

Conducting research and evaluation involves gathering the available facts necessary to a firmly based public relations effort, then narrowing the focus to those areas where changes can be effected. Library research, personal conversations, interviews with key people, and broad surveys of public opinion are some of the methods used in this process.

Defining the goals of a public relations campaign avoids waste of effort and money. At this point, plans are made for the amount of money to be spent on each main part of the project and for particular people to be employed to get the message across to selected audiences. For example, a campaign to bring more tourists to Hawaii might entail either sending a troupe of hula dancers and singers to perform at business luncheon meetings in the twenty-five largest American cities, or sending some Hawaiian swimming champions to perform at swimming meets around the country. The cooperation of people outside the public relations office must be obtained well in advance, and they must understand their job as ambassadors with a message.

Building working relationships is essential in public relations. Much of the effectiveness of campaigns depends upon favors given and received, information provided on the basis of personal friendship, and newspaper space or broadcast time made available because an editor or broadcaster likes and trusts a public relations person. Within a company, a public relations worker must sometimes work through the personnel department, the legal department, or the marketing department, and her or his effectiveness is in direct ratio to personal acceptability.

Writing and editing form a major part of public relations work because print is the communications medium most often used.

Among the writings of public relations people are press releases, brochures, pamphlets, booklets, annual reports, articles for trade magazines, statistics, survey results, technical data, newsletters, shareholder reports, and employee publications, as well as film scripts and speeches to be given by key personnel. Writing that is clear, lively, and effective in putting a message across will be an important part of any public relations work. As a matter of fact, many people who write well and want to be novelists eventually find themselves in public relations, where they are likely to be paid better (and more regularly) than they would be for writing novels.

Disseminating information to the appropriate editors of the relevant print and broadcast media is essential to communicating the messages of public relations to its publics. Keeping open the channels to these editors requires toleration, cooperation, and knowledge of the editors' needs and schedules. People in public relations do their best to be known, liked, and trusted by editors.

Producing communications includes all the techniques of art, photography, layout, typography, printing, cinema, television, and other means of putting the message across. Public relations workers must work with specialists in these fields and must know enough about the techniques to see that they are used with utmost effectiveness.

Developing special events may take thousands of forms. A state tourist promotion director may invite a dozen writers on a tour of her or his state in hopes of getting them to write and sell favorable articles. A state such as Virginia may host a party for several hundred writers and editors in New York and show a promotional film to increase their interest in Virginia. An essay contest on local history may be held for high school students in order to obtain newspaper publicity for local historical shrines when the winners are awarded their prizes. News conferences, travel shows, ski shows, boat shows, camping shows, canoe races, and many kinds of demonstrations of equipment also are used to promote travel. Public relations people may do the original planning for these events and then obtain the cooperation of the principals who speak, compete, or otherwise earn the interest of the public. Finally, the public relations people prepare news stories and reports about the event, easing the way for reporters to write their own stories.

Speaking in public is often important in public relations work. Many times a politician, company president, or celebrity, whose presence makes an event newsworthy, delivers a speech written by a public relations worker. A public relations worker needs to be an adept public speaker because he or she may often be asked to represent the client, company, or government by speaking at various types of meetings.

Public relations work is often frantic. If riots in a city cause prospective visitors to cancel reservations in the whole region, public relations workers must spread the word that all areas are not affected. An earthquake, a hurricane, a political coup, or an outbreak of disease can cause similar reactions and must be countered by public relations efforts. Such crises may involve work, travel during personal time to the site of the difficulty, and statements from authorities to be quoted to the press. An airplane crash always gets headlines and inevitably causes a drop in bookings on the airline. Public relations people for the carrier have to work around the clock for weeks after a crash, trying to restore the reputation of the carrier in the minds of the traveling public.

Ideally a public relations program is based on solid research, evaluation of facts, and determination of goals and schedules. Its various steps are planned for a period of a year to several years in advance.

Consider, for example, an island in the Caribbean or Mediterranean, for which a U.S. public relations agency is engaged to promote tourism. The island has only one hotel, small and very luxurious, but it has an ambitious construction program. In the first year, the agency might arrange visits by a number of celebrities to the one hotel, to build it up in the public mind as a "jet-set hideaway." As the island constructed the necessary infrastructure for development (water, sewage, and utility systems), the agency would report these items in the professional travel press, so travel agents would be reminded constantly of a new mass market to come. As new hotels were completed, the agency and the hotels would cooperate in holding highly publicized opening parties and celebrations, and shortly thereafter they would bring hundreds of travel agents on free or low-cost familiarization tours. Then package deals with airlines, hotels, and other services might be developed and publicized. Meanwhile, articles about the island's food would be sent to food editors; articles on crafts, history, sports, architecture, native habits, shows, and anything of news interest would go to other appropriate editors. The volume of news releases that can keep flooding out continually about even a little island is staggering.

This volume of press releases causes another problem. Every day, travel editors on metropolitan newspapers receive one or two mailbags full of publicity material. They cannot possibly print more than 1 percent of it, so the public relations writer has to use a lot of ingenuity to make releases and pictures distinctive enough to persuade an editor to even look at them.

Education and Training

The young person aiming toward a professional career in public relations should consider graduation from college essential. Many of today's top people in the field arrived by way of journalism, and they consider a degree in journalism, plus a year or two of experience on a newspaper, the best preparation for the field. However, specific education for public relations has been expanding rapidly. Many colleges and universities offered at least one course in public relations, and more than two hundred colleges had degree programs or special curricula in which public relations was an important part of a student's course of study. In addition, there are more than 220 chapters of the Public Relations Student Society of America on campuses nationwide.

Journalism or mass communications schools or departments administer most public relations programs. The Accrediting Council on Education in Journalism and Mass Communications (the ACEJMC) is the only agency authorized to accredit such schools or departments. Collegiate public relations curricula may be found in schools of journalism, communications, education, or business administration. Programs leading to a doctorate or a master's degree in public relations are now offered in more than sixty institutions.

In addition, an accreditation program—The Universal Accreditation Program—was formed in January 1998. The purpose of accreditation is to unify and advance the profession by identifying those who have demonstrated broad knowledge, experience, and professional judgment in the field. The program seeks to improve public relations practice. The designation Accredited in Public Relations (APR) signifies a high professional level of experience and competence.

Earnings and Job Outlook

According to a Public Relations Society of America study, salaries in public relations fall into a very broad range. The median range for public relations personnel is $53,000, a $4,000 increase from 1995. In 1999, salaries ranged from $28,000 to $147,000.

The job prospects outlook for public relations workers is favorable because the industry keeps growing as businesses add public relations departments and independent agencies expand their activities. According to the Bureau of Labor Statistics, jobs for public relations specialists are expected to increase by 36.1 percent between 2000 and 2010.

Sources of Information

Brochures on careers in public relations are available from the following organizations:

The Accrediting Council on Education in Journalism and Mass
    Communications (ACEJMC)
Stauffer-Flint Hall
1435 Jayhawk Blvd.
Lawrence, KS 66045-7575
ku.edu/~acejmc/index.html

ACEJMC is the agency that is responsible for the evaluation of professional journalism and mass communications programs in colleges and universities.

Canadian Public Relations Society, Inc. (CPRS)
One Yonge St., Ste. 1801
Toronto, ON
Canada M5E 1W7
cprstoronto.com

The CPRS represents more than eighteen hundred public relations and communications professionals in Canada.

PR and Marketing Network
1201 Seven Locks Rd., Ste. 300
Potomac, MD 20854
prandmarketing.com

PR and Marketing Network holds PR and marketing seminars, publishes newsletters and E-letters, holds award programs, and does custom publishing.

Public Relations Society of America
33 Irving Pl.
New York, NY 10003
prsa.org

Public Relations Student Society of America
33 Irving Pl.
New York, NY 10003
prssa.org

The declared purpose of PRSSA is to cultivate a favorable and mutually advantageous relationship between students and professional public relations practitioners.

Travel Industry Association (TIA)
1100 New York Ave. NW, Ste. 450
Washington, DC 20005-3934
tia.org

TIA is a nonprofit association that represents and speaks for the common interests and concerns of all components of the U.S. travel industry. It publishes *Travel Industry Public Relations Handbook*, an easy to read, step-by-step "how to" guide to eight important areas of travel and tourism public relations written by travel and tourism public relations professionals in the field.

7

RECREATION AND AMUSEMENT

SOME OF THE fastest-growing jobs in the tourism industry are in the recreation and amusement fields. In 2000 there were more than 1.7 million people working for approximately 102,000 establishments classified in the amusement and recreation fields. A large percentage of these jobs are directly related to travel and tourism. Basically, any activity that occupies a traveler's time is part of the amusement and recreation fields in the travel and tourism industry. These would include employment relating to fitness, boating, hunting, fishing, white-water adventures, amusement parks, museums, gaming, and in the entertainment industries such as theater or musical events.

Fitness has been a prime concern of North Americans and Europeans since the early 1980s. Hotels around the world now have running tracks and health clubs as standard facilities. Tennis, skiing, and other active sports attract more and more people. Golf vacations continue to rise. The Travel Industry Association (TIA) found that one in eight U.S. travelers played golf on a one-way trip of at least one hundred miles in 2000. Special interest travel such as adventure travel including off-road biking, mountain climbing, scuba diving, bird-watching, sailing, or canoeing is fashionable. Increasing leisure time has led to the proliferation of resorts and sports areas and the growth of the National Park System, as well as state and local parks. In 2000 the number of visitors to state parks broke records: 766 million visits occurred in the 4,710 areas operated by America's state park agencies. Overnight stays in parks, campgrounds, group lodges, resort facilities, and marinas were recorded in 1999 at 61.8 million. The consequence of the proliferation of these types of travel vacations has increased the demand for recreation leaders and administrators. In 1972 there were 55,000 recreation workers in year-round jobs; by 2000 recreation and fitness workers held about 427,000 jobs and many additional workers held summer jobs in this occupation. In 2000 about 63 percent of those employed in this field were recreation workers; the rest were fitness trainers and aerobics instructors. Of those with year-round jobs as recreation workers, more than one-third worked in park and recreation departments of municipal and county governments. The Canadian Parks/Recreation Association stated in 1984: "Recreation stands out as a career with a stable future."

Public and private support of recreation, although expanding rapidly now, is far from new. The stadium in ancient Greece, the amphitheater in Rome, public gardens, parks, zoos, swimming pools, baths, playgrounds, gymnasiums, opera houses, theaters, dance halls, athletic fields—all attest to people's inveterate devotion to recreation.

Since World War II, the number of hours in the average worker's week has been reduced, vacations have become longer, more holidays have been observed, and the moving of holidays to

Mondays or Fridays to lengthen the weekends has increased holiday travel.

In 1978 the U.S. National Park Service more than doubled the amount of land under its jurisdiction, to over 87 million acres in 384 parks. Many states also have set aside more land for parks, and commercial campgrounds and recreational vehicle (RV) parks have sprung up around many national and state parks to accommodate constantly overflowing crowds of campers. The National Association of RV Parks and Campgrounds states that in 1999, there were more than seventy-five million camper nights occupying one million RV sites. The industry's total revenue was just under $6 billion. Trends include increase in Internet usage at RV sites, water amenities at campgrounds, the attraction of noncampers and minority campers in the Northeast and Southwest, and a growing number of single females and single parents attracted to the social settings of campgrounds. In addition, employment at parks and campgrounds is shifting from teen and college students to older retirees looking for a more nomadic lifestyle.

As a consequence of this growth, completely new industries have been established to manufacture recreation vehicles, houseboats, camping gear, snow skis and water skis, hang gliders, and dozens of other kinds of recreation equipment. New recreational villages have sprung up—second-home and time-share condominium communities adjacent to ski areas, beaches, golf courses, tennis compounds, and primitive forests. All of these developments explain why the need for recreation workers is expanding so rapidly.

Job Responsibilities

The job responsibilities of those working in the recreation and amusement industries are outlined below.

Recreation

What specific jobs do recreation workers perform? They teach dancing and lead social get-togethers to help people meet each other at resorts. They lead calisthenic sessions on beaches and in gymnasiums, aiding people in keeping fit or losing weight. They serve as lifeguards; swimming, tennis, and golf instructors; and coaches for all sorts of athletic teams. They also lead singing groups and impromptu bands and orchestras, and they enlist acting talent and put on plays or musical dramas at resorts.

Some recreation workers concentrate on activities with certain age groups; for instance, teaching skiing to children ages three years and up, or keeping senior citizens busy with checkers and other sedentary activities. Many recreation workers teach handcrafts such as leatherwork, beadwork, basket weaving, macramé, batik, sewing, crocheting, and model building.

Recreation workers can be divided into three major groups according to their responsibilities. In the first group, made up of camp counselors and recreation leaders, the work consists of teaching people to do things they can enjoy in their leisure time and leading them in sports and games.

The second group consists of specialists in particular activities. In a large camp for young people, one specialist might spend all of her or his time teaching people how to make things out of leather, holding several classes each day. Another such specialist is the golf professional at a resort or country club. Recreation workers who have enough experience and enough capital sometimes start their own businesses such as camps, hobby shops, outfitters, trail-guide services, boat-rental services, white-water rafting services, and craft instruction schools.

Above these two groups are members of the third group, the supervisors and administrators of recreation programs, summer camps, shipboard passenger activity programs; and the directors of city parks and recreation departments and of leisure programs for nonprofit organizations, corporations, institutions, and the armed services.

Recreation administration involves major responsibility for planning and administering recreation and park programs to meet the needs and interests of the area served. Responsibilities include budgeting, trend forecasting, marketing, and other promotional techniques to attract participants to their recreation programs. Job titles include director of recreation and parks, recreation supervisor, recreation center director, recreation leader, recreation worker, and park planner.

In natural resource and park management, responsibilities are as diverse as wildlife management, park management, soil conservation, watershed management, and forestry. Job titles include park ranger, park police, park manager, or wildlife manager.

Today there are more than twelve thousand day and resident camps of varying types and lengths. Each summer more than ten million children and adults take advantage of these organized recreational and educational opportunities. Camp management requires skill, vision, and innovative strategies to be successful. Camps vary by style and format to meet many interests. Outdoor activities of hiking, swimming, sports and games, arts and crafts, and nature awareness are offered; some have special emphasis on programs such as horseback riding, water sports, music, or adventure challenge activities. Summer camps employ more than one million adults to work as counselors, program/activity leaders, unit and program directors/supervisors, and in support services roles such as maintenance, administration, food service, and health care.

The American Gaming Association (AGA) reports that in 2001 there were more than 434 commercial casinos operating in eleven states, directly employing more than 364,484 people with revenues of $25.6 billion. AGA also reports that 30 percent of U.S. households gamble at a casino, making an average of 5.4 trips during the year. In addition, during the past decade, the casino workforce has increased more than 79 percent, with the creation of seventeen thousand new jobs in the commercial casino industry. Jobs range from blackjack or poker dealer to behind-the-scenes jobs as pit clerk, cage cashier, slot technician, or surveillance officer.

Amusement Parks

Amusement parks in North America had sunk to a low ebb—notorious for their filthy food and atmosphere, pickpockets, confidence men, and dangerous, unsafe rides—when Walt Disney launched Disneyland in California in 1955. Disneyland revolutionized the industry. Everything was kept spic and span; blooming flowers and shrubs were everywhere. Most of the personnel in contact with the public were wholesome high school and college students who were friendly and helpful. Engineering ingenuity was put to work to design new rides and other excitements and to improve old ones. All uniforms were clean, neat, and colorful. Something of particular interest was offered for all ages.

Large theme parks and water parks can now be found in every state in the United States. Many of these parks have hotels in or adjacent to them, making it convenient for families. It is estimated that a total of 450 parks in North America generated total attendance of more than 317 million in 2000 and produced an economic impact of $9.6 billion. The U.S. theme park revenue will continue to grow, estimated by PricewaterhouseCoopers at 5.1 percent through 2005. An interesting fact is that over the next ten years, the U.S. population age forty-five and over will grow considerably. This age group does not traditionally have a burning desire to visit a traditional theme park. Park operators, looking for new markets and revenue, are finding ways to target this market—made up primarily of adult couples without children—with adult-oriented rides and golf courses, upscale hotels, restaurants, spas, and nighttime entertainment.

Employment at amusement parks is a two-tier affair. There is a small cadre of permanent staff and a huge horde of part-timers—more than two hundred thousand in North America during the summer. The permanent crew includes executives in charge of maintenance, operations, sales, purchasing, advertising, public relations, food, and rides and their small full-time staffs. Descriptions for permanent jobs vary. They can range from project scheduler, whose responsibilities include "the development, implementation and maintenance of plans and schedules for attraction projects from conception through completion"; to general manager of a $7 million start-up leisure attraction; to park operations manager, who is responsible for "the management of multiple amusement parks and entertainment facilities."

A few parks in warm areas are open all year, but most, influenced by climate and school vacations, operate only in summer and on spring and fall weekends. All have cyclical busy and slow seasons.

Requirements

In such a broad industry as recreation and amusement, requirements for the many types of jobs naturally vary from job to job and from employer to employer. Employment conditions for recreation workers are usually very pleasant; they are helping people to enjoy life and to learn simple skills that give a feeling of accomplishment. Generally a recreation worker should be an outgoing, gregarious person who is interested in other people and eager to help and to teach. The work should bring pleasure to the recreation professional, because he or she must work when most other people are at leisure—evenings, weekends, and the summer vacation months.

Education and Training

More than 40 percent of workers in the recreation and amusement industries have no formal education past high school. The services jobs are traditionally filled by young, unskilled workers the majority of time during seasonal months.

To obtain a year-round position in recreation, considerable experience is highly desirable, as is graduation from at least a two-year—or preferably, a four-year—college. Varying degrees of certification are required depending on the job and employer. In a physical fitness facility, a fitness trainer or aerobics instructor may require a specific type of certification by the facility owner. For a full-time position as a recreation administrator, applicants are usually college graduates with a major in parks, recreation, and leisure services. Persons with academic preparation in parks, recreation, or leisure studies; physical education; fitness management; and related fields generally have better prospects for career advancement. The profession of directing recreation is a young one that is growing rapidly; as it grows, educational requirements will become more stringent. A person with foresight and determination will complete four years of college and go on to obtain a master's degree, and perhaps even a doctorate, to avoid being prevented from advancing later because of a lack of formal educational credentials.

Many recreation workers specializing in music, drama, and art have graduate degrees. Graduate work might well include courses such as business administration, since program directors must prepare budgets, allocate funds, and conduct their recreation programs in a businesslike fashion. Other graduate courses should concentrate mainly on the recreation professional's specific area of interest.

Camp directors are required to have some know-how and background in technical fields such as nutrition, food service, facility design and maintenance, risk management, marketing, and personnel and business management. This job also necessitates the blending of the principles of social group work, recreation, child development, physical education, health and wellness, psychology, and education.

In the amusement park industry, for temporary or seasonal workers, the parks tend to look for youth, wholesomeness, and an outgoing personality. Education is helpful but not important. For permanent positions, however, knowledge counts—a degree in business administration, public relations, advertising, restaurant management, or food service (or perhaps hotel and restaurant management if the park owns a hotel) is an advantage. If you want a career in amusement parks, go after a college degree, and gain valuable experience during your time off by working in several departments of various parks.

Earnings and Job Outlook

Earnings in the recreation and amusement industries are generally low, reflecting the large numbers of part-time and seasonal jobs.

Nonsupervisory workers in these services positions averaged $262 a week in 2000, compared with $474 in the private industry. Median hourly earnings of fitness trainers and aerobics instructors in all industries in 2000 were $10.96, and the top 10 percent earned $25.98 or more. In 2000, earnings of these workers in the miscellaneous amusement and recreation services industry, which includes commercial fitness clubs, were $12.22 an hour; fitness trainers and aerobics instructors in civic and social associations earned $9.03. Earnings for successful self-employed personal trainers can be much higher. Median hourly earnings of amusement and recreation attendants in the recreation and amusement industry in 2000 were $6.63. Benefits in amusement and theme parks include free passes to the park, transportation to and from work, housing, discounts on park merchandise, and even sometimes scholarships.

According to the Bureau of Labor Statistics, jobs for recreation and amusement services workers are expected to increase by approximately 35 percent between 2000 and 2010. These jobs are ranked as one of the highest-growth occupations in this ten-year period. Increasing income, leisure time, and the recognition of the health benefits of being fit contribute to this high-growth services industry. An increase in the average age of the U.S. population will lead to an increase in markets that cater to an elderly clientele, such as golf courses or cruise ships.

Sources of Information

American Alliance for Health, Physical Education, Recreation, and
    Dance (AAHPERD)
1900 Association Dr.
Reston, VA 22091
aahperd.org

AAHPERD is the largest organization of professionals supporting and assisting those involved in physical education, leisure, fitness, dance, health promotion, and education.

American Camping Association (ACA)
Bradford Woods
5000 State Road 67N
Martinsville, IN 46151
acacamps.org

The ACA is a community of more than six thousand camping professionals.

American Gaming Association (AGA)
555 Thirteenth St. NW, Ste. 1010 East
Washington, DC 20004
americangaming.org

The AGA represents the commercial casino entertainment industry.

Canadian Association for Health, Physical Education, Recreation, and Dance (CAHPERD)
403-2197 Riverside Dr.
Ottawa, ON
Canada K1H 7X3
cahperd.ca

CAHPERD is a national, charitable, voluntary-sector organization whose primary concern is to influence the healthy development of children and youth by advocating for quality, school-based physical and health education.

Canadian Parks/Recreation Association
404-2197 Riverside Dr.
Ottawa, ON
Canada K1H 7X3
cpra.ca

CPRA is a national voice for the Canadian parks and recreation industry.

International Association of Amusement Parks and Attractions
    (IAAPA)
1448 Duke St.
Alexandria, VA 22314
iaapa.org

IAAPA exists to foster the highest degree of professionalism within the amusement industry, to promote the market for its goods and services, to gather and disseminate information on the industry, and to represent the interests of the industry before government.

National Amusement Park Historical Association (NAPHA)
P.O. Box 83
Mt. Prospect, IL 60056

NAPHA is an international organization dedicated to the preservation and enjoyment of the amusement and theme park industry—past, present, and future.

National Association of RV Parks and Campgrounds (ARVC)
113 Park Ave.
Falls Church, VA 22046
arvc.org

ARVC is the trade association representing the commercial RV park and campground industry throughout the United States.

National Recreation and Park Association (NRPA)
22377 Belmont Ridge Rd.
Ashburn, VA 20148
nrpa.org

NRPA's goal is to promote public awareness and support for recreation, park, and leisure services.

Parks Canada
25 Eddy St.
Hull, Quebec
Canada K1A 0M5
http://parkscanada.pch.gc.ca

Parks Canada's mandate is to protect and present nationally significant examples of Canada's natural and cultural heritage and to foster public understanding, appreciation, and enjoyment in ways that ensure their ecological and commemorative integrity for present and future generations.

8

TRAVEL WRITING

IN ENGLISH SLANG a few generations ago, a "traveler's tale" meant a tall story—a highly colored and exaggerated account of adventures in exotic and faraway lands. Most of the world's literatures have included such reports. Homer's *Odyssey*, dating from about 850 B.C., not only relates the adventures of Odysseus (Ulysses) over the twenty years it took him to come home from the Trojan War, but also describes accurately many parts of the Mediterranean world that he visited.

One of the world's most fascinating travel classics is *The Book of Marco Polo*. Fortunately for the world, this Venetian man of action, after his epochal journeys across Asia and his twenty-four years in the service of Kublai Khan, was taken prisoner in a war between Venice and Genoa. Using his carefully written travel notebooks, in 1298 he dictated to a fellow captive, the scribe Rustigielo of Pisa, the book that disclosed Cathay to Europe. Christopher Columbus had a copy of this book and made notations on more than seventy pages. His object, when he sailed in 1492, was to reach Marco Polo's Cathay.

Another monumental travel writer was Richard Hakluyt of England, who became archdeacon of Westminster and is buried in Westminster Abbey. Between 1582 and 1600 he wrote several books, chief of which is his *Principal Navigations, Voyages, and Discoveries of the English Nation*, which describes all the great sea expeditions of English captains to America, the Arctic, the Pacific, and around the world.

If only some chronicler had joined the fishing expeditions of early Portuguese, French, English, and Scandinavian fishermen, we might know much more about ancient landings in North America. It is suspected that there was fishing from European ships on the Grand Banks off Newfoundland and Nova Scotia as far back as a thousand years ago.

The first important analysis of the United States and its life is *De la democratie en Amerique (Democracy in America)*, published in 1835 by Comte Alexis de Tocqueville. Sent to examine the U.S. penitentiary system for the French government, de Tocqueville wrote his report on prisons, and then, in *Democracy in America*, he described American life with such penetration as had never been applied before, and seldom since. He perceived that the great difference between Europe and America was the American insistence on equality, and he showed how this affected every facet of life, from emergent literature to science, religion, philosophy, the arts, language, business, the family, the military, and manners. He didn't care much for our ancestors' manners, but he foresaw that the influence of democracy would bring about the emancipation of women.

De Tocqueville's work would not be considered travel writing by some persons—those who believe that travel writing concerns itself solely with the traveler's transportation, accommodations, shopping, and recreation. But, in reality, this is the very best kind of travel writing, because de Tocqueville delivers that most precious gift—insight.

The insight of the travel writer can bring the reader to feel kinship with people of another land and another race by showing the universal emotions and motivations behind customs that seem strange, even bizarre. An alert travel writer is always attuned to the subtle emanations of a new place and its people. Every bit of feeling that a place arouses in a travel writer must be savored, perhaps analyzed, but certainly fully realized, so that the writer can express it in a way that makes the reader feel it as well.

Two men who strongly influenced the development of travel guidebooks as we know them today were John Murray of London and Karl Baedeker of Koblenz, Germany. John Murray (1808–1892) was the third of a distinguished line of publishers, all bearing the same name. He wrote a series of travel handbooks on the Netherlands, Belgium, France, the Rhine, South Germany, and Switzerland.

Karl Baedeker (1801–1859) started a printing plant in Koblenz in 1827. Under an arrangement with John Murray, he published a pocket-sized guidebook on the Rhine, Belgium, and the Netherlands in 1839. He subsequently brought out guides covering most of Europe and parts of North America and Asia. These books were so reliable and thorough that the name *Baedeker* became a synonym for the word "guidebook." The era of exaggerated "traveler's tales" had ended. Baedeker started the practice of marking with one or more stars in his books places of special interest or attraction, so travelers with little time could determine quickly what to see. "Starred in *Baedeker*" soon came to mean "well worth seeing."

These *Baedeker* guides were published from the beginning in German, French, and English, and this helped them to gain extremely wide readership.

Modern Travel Guidebooks

In our own time, the mantle of Baedeker graced the shoulders of Eugene Fodor, a native Hungarian who became an American citizen. He was editing travel books by 1936 and began publishing *Fodor's* guides in Paris after World War II. He moved his headquarters to the United States in the 1960s and retired in the late 1970s. For each *Fodor's* guide, authorship is generally shared by a number of writers and researchers—whenever possible, experts residing in the country described by the book. Fodor has died, but his guides live on.

Quite different are the highly personal guidebooks exemplified by Myra Waldo's *Travel and Motoring Guide to Europe* and *Fielding's Travel Guide to Europe* (by Temple Fielding). These popular guidebooks, revised annually, depend for their attraction on the readers' confidence that they can rely upon the taste and preferences of Myra Waldo and the late Temple Fielding.

Arthur Frommer, after traveling through Europe with his wife as inexpensively as possible, wrote *Europe on $5 a Day*, an inexpensive paperback book. The title's assertion that travel could be very inexpensive doubtless inspired many Americans to visit Europe. For millions of young people, it was a bible of essential information, carried around Europe until it was dog-eared and tattered. It was such a success that Frommer started a publishing house, which now keeps a number of authors busy writing and updating more than fifty titles. A single writer or a team of two writers writes each book. Having achieved fame as a travel writer, then as a travel-book publisher, Frommer went on to become a package-tour operator and hotel impresario.

For many readers, escapist literature offers excitement and exotic scenes that take them out of their daily routines. Travel books do this with descriptions of true adventure in jungle exploration or mountain climbing, treasure hunting or visiting natives of lost civilizations, archaeological exploration or sailing trips across an ocean on a raft. This kind of escapist nonfiction permits armchair travel and is at the opposite end of the spectrum of travel writing from the step-by-step *Baedeker*.

In between these opposites are many kinds of books on outdoor life, hunting and fishing, camping, ecology, folklore, local crafts, transportation, skiing, boating, history, cruising, flying, gliding, and so forth. Some of these are written to amaze or amuse the reader, others to give the reader practical advice and instruction.

As travel has become more widespread, the amount of travel coverage in magazines and newspapers has increased. Travel is a major interest, and people do more traveling every year. Another reason for the increase in the number of travel articles is that travel advertising has been increasing from year to year. A magazine or newspaper carrying a great deal of travel advertising must carry a commensurate amount of travel writing; otherwise, readers do not look at the advertising. If a Sunday newspaper's travel section had only advertisements, most people would discard it unread.

Freelance Travel Writing

Making a living as a freelance travel writer is becoming increasingly difficult. Newspapers, whose Sunday travel sections had been the largest market for travel articles, are becoming fewer. As newspapers decline in number, however, all kinds of specialized magazines spring up. They do not use as many travel articles as the newspapers had, and their standards are often higher, but magazines of many kinds use travel articles in hopes of attracting travel advertising. This has increased the number of jobs for staff writers and editors.

A growing threat to freelance travel writers is the decision by a few of the most prestigious magazines to refuse articles generated by sponsored trips, as a few top newspapers did in the early 1970s.

Although travel writing is important to readers, and therefore essential to magazines and newspapers, it is not a lucrative field for the writers. The reason is an ancient economic one—the law of supply and demand. So many people are willing to write articles on travel for little or nothing, and public relations people supply so many free articles and pictures, that an editor on a slim budget may decide to buy no articles at all, relying solely on free material.

During the economic slowdown of the mid-1970s, when newspapers suffered a shortage of newsprint (paper) and greatly increased costs (ink and labor), many newspapers that had been regular buyers of travel articles from freelancers completely stopped buying. They had their travel editors write articles, they used free articles from public relations sources, and they used articles provided by the wire services at very low cost. This is happening again, as many publications fold due to the economic slowdown.

The Society of American Travel Writers (SATW) was founded in 1956. SATW has approximately 1,460 members, and its primary goals are first, to promote responsible journalism; second, to provide professional support and development for its members;

and third, to encourage the conservation and preservation of travel resources worldwide. Throughout the years, SATW members have seen changes in the travel writing profession.

Adele Malott, current SATW president, says of the changes:

> Indeed, travel writing has changed in the last decade or so and will continue to change along with the world itself. With the extended use of new technology such as computers and the Internet, a travel writer has worldwide research available on his or her desktop and can reach far afield to find new markets for material created. The challenge is being able to keep up with all the new developments and learn to use them. I have always believed that a writer who sells well is one with a specialty and I think that will continue to be the case. Writers who know the psychographics of a travel entity—the student, the family, the senior, the doctor, the professor—will always be able to find a market for their work, primarily because they can provide information beyond the norm.

In 1980 a second national travel writers' organization was formed—the Travel Journalists Guild (TJG). Composed solely of freelance travel writers and travel photographers, its establishment was necessitated by the fact that freelance objectives could not be pursued in the SATW because they conflicted with the policies that travel editors in SATW had to enforce for their publishers. The founding president of TJG, Bern Keating, performed a signal service for all American freelance writers by obtaining the introduction in the Senate of a bill to amend the copyright law so that publishers would not be permitted to buy other than first serial rights of articles, unless other rights were paid for. The bill had a hearing but did not reach the Senate floor. Many other writers', photographers', and artists' groups joined ranks in support of the amendment, and the fight goes on. Membership is kept small and highly professional.

Travel writing, for most freelance writers, does not earn enough to cover the costs of the necessary travel. Recognizing this (and hoping to obtain coverage of their attractions or facilities) airlines, resorts, hotels, railroads, cruise lines, and local and national governments often invite travel writers on press trips and cover part or all of their expenses.

In the early 1970s, several prestigious newspapers declared they would no longer buy travel articles based on "sponsored" trips. One editor went so far as to say this was a dishonest way of obtaining information for an article, despite the fact that his publication pays quite low rates, demands "magazine quality" articles, and pays no expenses. Under these conditions, of course, a travel writer specializing in faraway places must have other income in order to write for these papers. This cuts out the professional freelancer, and, in fact, leaves this article market to those who do not depend on travel writing for their income—business travelers, pleasure travelers with a flair for writing, and others for whom travel writing is a sideline.

The same newspapers that reject press trips as unethical accept free tickets to plays, ballets, concerts, and sports events for their theater critics, dance critics, music critics, and sportswriters. They also pay the expenses of any reporter who must travel to cover a story.

Another difficulty for people trying to become full-time professional freelance travel writers is that the "star" system is in effect at most of the best magazines. An editor wants to publish as many articles by celebrities as possible, so their names can be printed on the cover to help sell the magazine. This makes it difficult for a newcomer to break into the field and to sell enough articles to keep going.

This look at the problems shows that freelance travel writing is, in general, an insecure field. For those with talent and persistence, however, it is a fascinating way to earn a living.

Travel Editors

A position as travel editor of a magazine or newspaper is much more secure than that of a freelancer. There is a regular salary, there are regular hours in the publication's offices, and, in the case of most metropolitan newspapers, there is a union contract to regulate working conditions. The Newspaper Guild, the union for reporters and editors, has been quite militant about obtaining good salaries and other benefits for its members.

Travel writing and travel editing are generally not recognized as specialties open to beginning reporters and editors in the newspaper world, so the neophyte must begin as a general reporter or copy editor. As more educational institutions develop curricula in Transportation, Travel, and Tourism (TTT); Hospitality and Tourism Management; or Hospitality, Restaurant, and Institutional Management, newspapers may begin to place these graduates in assignments that cover these subjects.

There are so few magazine travel editors that it is difficult to generalize about them, but it can be said that a college education is required for such work. Some travel editors are journalism graduates, but many are graduates in fine arts. For both newspapers and magazines, the master's degree is becoming increasingly necessary.

The work of a travel editor varies greatly from one publication to another. On some newspapers and magazines, the travel editor is actually the sole travel writer. Richard Joseph, for example, was travel editor of *Esquire* from 1946 until he died while on a trip in the late 1970s. He generally wrote two articles for each issue, and *Esquire* seldom bought any other travel articles.

To become any kind of a travel writer, editor, or broadcaster today, an undergraduate college education is essential, and graduate degrees help. A travel photographer does not need college training but must have a great deal of technical expertise, as well as flair for the work. The competition in this work is very stiff—a magazine editor selecting photographs to illustrate an article often will have one to two hundred or more offered, of which only one to five may be used.

Sources of Information

American Society of Journalists and Authors (ASJA)
1501 Broadway, Ste. 302
New York, NY 10036
asja.org/index9.php

ASJA is the nation's leading organization of independent nonfiction writers.

Association of Women in Communications (AWAC)
(formerly Women in Communications)
780 Ritchie Hwy., Ste. 28-S
Severna Park, MD 21146
womcom.org/indexie.html

AWAC is a professional organization that champions the advancement of women across all communications disciplines by recognizing excellence, promoting leadership, and positioning its members at the forefront of the evolving communications era.

Canadian Newspaper Association (CNA)
321 Bloor St., East
Toronto, ON
Canada M4W 1E7
cna-acj.ca/default.asp?language=english

CNA is a nonprofit organization, representing one hundred Canadian daily newspapers (English and French).

The Dow Jones Newspaper Fund, Inc. (DJNF)
P.O. Box 300
Princeton, NJ 08540
http://djnewspaperfund.dowjones.com/fund

DJNF is a nonprofit foundation supported by the Dow Jones Foundation and provides internships and scholarships to college students, career literature, fellowships for high school journalism teachers and publications' advisers, and training for college journalism instructors.

East West News Bureau (EWNB) and the North American Travel
   Journalists Association (NATJA)
531 Main St., #902
El Segundo, CA 90245

EWNB/NATJA is a professional association dedicated to the travel, food, wine, and hospitality industries. EWNB's goals are to support high-quality professional journalism, to promote travel and leisure activities to the public, to encourage international collaboration among its industries, and to honor the excellence of journalists throughout the world.

The Newspaper Guild (TNG)
8611 Second Ave.
Silver Spring, MD 20910
newsguild.org

The TNG is a media union. Wage scale information is found on its website.

Periodical Writers Association of Canada (PWAC)
54 Wolseley St.
Toronto, ON
Canada M5T 1A5
web.net/~pwac

The PWAC mandate is to protect and promote the rights and careers of independent, freelance periodical writers.

Society of American Travel Writers (SATW)
1500 Sunday Dr., Ste. 102
Raleigh, NC 27607
satw.org

SATW is a tax-exempt professional association whose purpose is to promote responsible journalism, provide professional support and development for its members, and encourage the conservation and preservation of travel resources worldwide.

Travel Journalists Guild (TJG)
P.O. Box 10643
Chicago, IL 60610
tjgonline.com

TJG is a select group of freelance writers, photographers, filmmakers, and artists who specialize in travel worldwide.

Colleges and Universities Offering Degrees or Sequences in the Field of Travel

THE TRAVEL INDUSTRY has finally been recognized as one of the most important in North America. This realization, along with the industry's burgeoning demand for trained people, has caused a tripling since 1980 in the number of colleges offering degrees or sequences in travel-related fields. This growth is occurring so rapidly that it is not possible to include all the colleges and universities in this appendix. Visit your public library and consult the reference books listed below for the most current names and addresses of institutions. These references are updated annually, so make sure you are using the most recent editions.

Look for universities, four-, and two-year colleges that offer degrees in travel and tourism management; hospitality; hotel, motel, and restaurant management; recreation; and transportation.

Antonoff, Steven R. *College Finders*. New York: Fawcett Books, 1999.

Barron's Profiles of American Colleges. Hauppage, N.Y.: Division
   of Barron's Educational Series, Inc., 2002.
National College Databank. Princeton, N.J.: Peterson's Guide to
   Career Colleges, 2002 (includes Canadian schools).
Straughn, Charles T., and Barbara Sue Lovejoy-Straughn. *Love-
   joy's College Guide*, 25th edition. New York: Arco, 1998.

If you have access to a computer and can connect to the Internet, do an online search. If you do not have a computer or are not
able to get online, your closest public library would be the place
to go. The librarians will be able to help you in your search.
   The following sites are helpful:

- **petersons.com.** *Peterson's Guide to Career Colleges*
- **career.org.** The Career College Association is a voluntary
  membership organization of private, postsecondary schools,
  institutes, colleges, and universities that provide career-
  specific educational programs.
- **collegeboard.com.** The College Board is a national nonprofit membership association whose mission is to prepare,
  inspire, and connect students to college and opportunity.
- **cthrc.ca/careerplan.shtml.** The Canadian Tourism Human
  Resource Council (CTHRC) is a national nonprofit organization that promotes and enhances professionalism in the
  Canadian tourism industry. The Career Planning section
  provides good information for getting a start in a tourism
  career. From cthrc.ca/youth_travelmap.shtml download the
  "Student's Travel Map—A Guide to Tourism Careers, Education, and Training" guide, which gives a concise overview
  of the tourism industry, highlights dynamic career choices

available within each sector of tourism, and provides information about tourism-focused education programs available in Canada.

There are excellent directories to travel schools and academic programs available through associations. The following are very helpful.

American Society of Travel Agents (ASTA)
1101 King St., Ste. 200
Alexandria, VA 22314
asta.org

National Tourism Foundation
546 E. Main St.
Lexington, KY 40508
ntfonline.org

The National Tourism Foundation has a list of seven hundred schools offering programs in travel-related fields. Through its website, ntfon line.org, click on "Careerlink." You will find a table of contents that lists tourism programs. The links will bring up the names and addresses of schools.

- ntfonline.org/careerlinks/display.cfm?data_id=111: Schools with certificate programs in tourism
- ntfonline.org/careerlinks/display.cfm?data_id=113: Schools with associate programs in tourism
- ntfonline.org/careerlinks/display.cfm?data_id=114: Schools with bachelor's degree programs in tourism

- ntfonline.org/careerlinks/display.cfm?data_id=115: Schools with master's degree programs in tourism
- ntfonline.org/careerlinks/display.cfm?data_id=116: Schools with doctorate degree programs in tourism
- ntfonline.org/careerlinks/display.cfm?data_id=117: International Guide Academy
- ntfonline.org/careerlinks/display.cfm?data_id=118: International Tour Management Institute
- ntfonline.org/careerlinks/display.cfm?data_id=119: The Travel School

International Council on Hotel, Restaurant, and Institutional
Education (I-CHRIE)
2613 N. Parham Rd., 2nd Fl.
Richmond, VA 23294
chrie.org

I-CHRIE is the global advocate of hospitality and tourism education for schools, colleges, and universities offering programs in hotel and restaurant management, foodservice management, and culinary arts. It publishes the *Guide to College Programs in Hospitality, Tourism, & Culinary Arts*, a resource for prospective students and industry employees seeking advancement through education, career counselors, corporate recruiters, and industry organizations.

Current recommended U.S. hospitality undergraduate programs in 2000–2001, as ranked by I-CHRIE's *Journal of Hospitality & Tourism Education* in its study "Top U.S. Hospitality Undergraduate Programs 2000–2001," include the following (listing copyright © I-CHRIE):

Boston University
School of Hospitality Administration
808 Commonwealth Ave.
Boston, MA 02215
bu.edu/hospitality

California Polytechnic University, Pomona
The Collins School of Hospitality Management
3801 W. Temple Ave.
Pomona, CA 91768
csupomona.edu/~cshm

Colorado State University
Department of Restaurant and Resort Management
Ft. Collins, CO 80523-1480
cnr.colostate.edu/nrrt

Florida International University
School of Hospitality Management
3000 NE 151st St.
North Miami, FL 33181
http://hospitality.fiu.edu

Florida State University
Dedman School of Hospitality
1 Champions Way, Rm. 4110
Tallahassee, FL 32306-2541
cob.fsu.edu/ha

Georgia State University
Cecil B. Day School of Hospitality
35 Broad St., Ste. 1215/University Plaza
Atlanta, GA 30303
robinson.gsu.edu/hospitality

Iowa State University
Department of Hotel, Restaurant, and Institutional Management
8A MacKay Hall
Ames, IA 50011-1120
fcs.iastate.edu/hrim

Johnson and Wales University
School of Hospitality Management
8 Abbott Park Pl.
Providence, RI 02903
jwu.edu/hosp/index.htm

Kansas State University
Department of Hotel, Restaurant, Institution Management, and
    Dietetics
103 Justin Hall
Dept. of HRIMD
Manhattan, KS 66506-1404
humec.ksu.edu/hrimd

Metropolitan State College of Denver
Department of Hospitality, Meeting, and Travel Administration
Plaza Bldg., Rm. 124
Auraria Higher Education Center
Denver, CO 80217-3362
mscd.edu/~hmt

Michigan State University
The School of Hospitality Management
232 Eppley Center
East Lansing, MI 48824
bus.msu.edu/shb

New Mexico State University
Department of Hotel and Restaurant Management
Box 30003, MSC 3HRTM
Las Cruces, NM 88003-0003
nmsu.edu

Niagara University
College of Hospitality and Tourism Management
Niagara University, NY 14109-2012
niagara.edu/hospitality

Northern Arizona University
School of Hotel and Restaurant Management
P.O. Box 5638
Flagstaff, AZ 86011-5638
nau.edu/hrm

Oklahoma State University
School of Hotel, Restaurant, and Tourism Management
210 HES West
Stillwater, OK 74078
http://osuhrad.org

Pennsylvania State University
School of Hotel, Restaurant, and Recreation Management
201 Mateer Bldg.
University Park, PA 16802-6501
hrrm.psu.edu

Purdue University
School of Hospitality and Tourism Management
1266 Stone Hall, Rm. 106
West Lafayette, IN 47907-1266
cfs.purdue.edu

Robert Morris University
Department of Hospitality and Tourism
Narrows Run Rd.
Corapolis, PA 15108-1189
rmu.edu

Texas Tech University
Department of Restaurant, Hotel, and Institutional Management
Box 41162
Lubbock, TX 79409-1162
hs.ttu.edu/enrhm/rhim

University of Central Florida
Rosen School of Hospitality Management
Office CH-302
Orlando, FL 32816-1450
hospitality.ucf.edu

University of Delaware
Department of Hotel, Restaurant, and Institutional Management
321 South College Ave.
Newark, DE 19716
udel.edu/hrim

University of Denver
School of Hotel, Restaurant, and Tourism Management
2030 E. Evans Ave.
Denver, CO 80208
dcb.du.edu/hrtm

University of Houston
The Conrad N. Hilton College of Hotel and Restaurant
    Management
Houston, TX 77204-3902
hrm.uh.edu

University of Massachusetts, Amherst
Department of Hotel, Restaurant, and Travel Administration
107 Flint Lab
Amherst, MA 01003-2710
umass.edu/hrta

University of Nevada, Las Vegas
The William F. Harrah College of Hotel Administration
4505 Maryland Pkwy., Box 456023
Las Vegas, NV 89154-6023
http://tca.unlv.edu

University of South Carolina
School of Hotel and Restaurant Management
Institute for Tourism Research
Columbia, SC 29208
aps.sc.edu/hrtm

Virginia Polytechnic Institute and State University
Department of Hospitality and Tourism Management
351 Wallace Hall
Blacksburg, VA 24061-0462
chre.vt.edu/htm/index.htm

Washington State University
Department of Hotel and Restaurant Administration
Pullman, WA 99164
cbe.wsu.edu/departments/hra

Widener University
School of Hospitality Management
One University Pl.
Chester, PA 19013
widener.edu/soh

Bibliography, Recommended Reading, and Websites

The following are good sources of information about the various aspects of the travel industry.

Bibliography

2001 Lodging Industry Profile. Washington, D.C.: American Hotel and Lodging Association, 2001.

2002 Annual Report for the Air Transport Association. Washington, D.C.: Air Transport Association, 2002.

"A Partner in U.S. Economic Growth." *What Is the International Council of Cruise Lines?* 15 July 2002: iccl.org/whoweare/index.html.

"About SATW." 10 July 2002: satw.org.

"Aviation Safety Inspector." 11 June 2002: faa.gov/careers/employment/asi.htm.

Becoming a Travel Agent. Alexandria, Va.: American Society of Travel Agents, 2002.

Benz, Matthew. "Park Industry Eyes Growth on Global Scale." *Amusement Business*, 2 July 2001: 1.

"Brief Amtrak History." 27 May 2002: amtrakhistoricalsociety.com.

Bzizek, Michael G., and Mahmood A. Khan. "Ranking of Hospitality Undergraduate Programs, 2000–2001." *Journal of Hospitality & Tourism Education.* August 2002: 5.

The Canadian Tourism Commission. *Who We Are and What We Do.* Ottawa: The Canadian Tourism Commission, February 2002.

"Careers in Public Relations." 6 June 2002: prsa.org/resources/profession/index.asp?ident=prof1.

Cockerell, Nancy. *World Travel & Tourism Demand in 2002.* London: International Tourism Exchange ITB Berlin, March 2002.

"Economic Impact of Travel and Tourism." *Economic Research.* April 2002: 9. July 2002: tia.org/travel/econimpact.asp.

Garvey, Jane F. "Planning for a Stronger Future." March 2002. 2 July 2002: api.faa.gov/conference/conference2002commercial/aoa.html.

"General Schedule Pay." 11 June 2002: usajobs.opm/gov/b5a.htm.

Henkin, Shepard, et al. *Opportunities in Hotel and Motel Management Careers.* Chicago, Ill.: VGM Career Books, 2000.

"Highlights." *U.S. Travel Agents Survey 2000.* January 2001. 12 June 2002: twcrossroads.com/agentsurvey2000/pages/message.html.

Kass, Daniel, and Sumiye Okubo. *U.S. Travel and Tourism Satellite Accounts for 1996 and 1997, Survey of Current Business.* Washington, D.C.: GPO, 2000.

Looking for a Career Where the Sky Is the Limit? Herndon, Va.: Air Line Pilots Association, 2001.

Merlino, Diane. *2000 Travel Counselor Magazine Salary Survey.* Wellesley, Mass.: Institute of Certified Travel Agents, 2001.

Opening a Travel Agency. Alexandria, Va.: American Society of Travel Agents, 2002.

"Profile of the U.S. Cruise Industry." *Cruise Industry Source Book.* 2001. 05 June 2002: cruising.org/press/sourcebook/profile_cruise_industry.htm.

"TIA Releases Forecast for Travel Volume and Spending." November 2001. 10 July 2002: tia.org/press/pressrec.asp?item=159.

Tourism Works for America, 10th annual edition, 2001. Washington, D.C.: Travel Industry Association of America, August 2001.

U.S. Bureau of Labor Statistics. *Career Guide to Industries, 2002–03.* Washington, D.C.: GPO, 2002.

U.S. Bureau of Labor Statistics. *Occupational Outlook Handbook.* Washington, D.C.: GPO, 2002.

"The U.S. Travel and Tourism Industry." *Tourism Talking Points.* April 2002. 10 July 2002: tia.org/tourism/talkingpoints.asp.

Yesawich, Pepperdine & Brown and Yankelovich Partners' 2002 National Travel Monitor. Orlando: Yesawich, Pepperdine & Brown, 2002.

Yesawich, Peter C. "Consumer Trends." *2002 Domestic Marketing for Travel and Tourism, Proceedings of the Travel Industry*

Association of America's Twenty-Seventh Annual Marketing Outlook Forum. January 2002: 125.

Recommended Reading

Backhausen, Marguerite. *Travelwriter Marketletter*. A monthly newsletter for travel writers: travelwriterml.com.

Bow, Sandra. *Working on Cruise Ships*, 2nd edition. Oxford, England: Vacation-Work Publishers, 1997.

Dial, Cynthia. *Teach Yourself Travel Writing*, London: Hodder & Stoughton Ltd., 2001.

Eberts, Marjorie, Linda Brother, and Margaret Gisler. *Careers in Travel, Tourism, and Hospitality*. Chicago, Ill.: VGM Career Books, 1997.

Farewell, Susan. *How to Make a Living as a Travel Writer*, 2nd edition. New York: Marlowe & Company, 1997.

Rubin, Karen. *Inside Secrets to Finding a Career in Travel*. Indianapolis: JIST Publishing, 2001.

"Student's Travel Map—A Guide to Tourism Careers, Education, and Training." Ottawa, Canada: The Canadian Tourism Human Resource Council (CTHRC), 2000: cthrc.ca/youth_travelmap.shtml.

Zobel, Louise Purwin. *The Travel Writer's Handbook: How to Write and Sell Your Own Travel Experiences*, 5th edition. Chicago: Surrey Books, 2002.

Websites

In addition to the websites listed in each chapter, here are some general websites to research for travel employment.

- Human Resources Development Canada: hrdc.gc.ca

    HRDC's mission is to enable Canadians to participate fully in the workplace and the community. The "Jobs, Workers, Training, and Careers" section provides links to information on programs and services related to job search and career development. For additional job search and career-related information, you can consult the Jobs, Workers, Training, and Careers website (http://jobsetc.ca) from the Government of Canada's website.
- Tourism Work Web: tourismworkweb.com/index.jhtml

    Tourism Work Web is Canada's premier online recruiting and resource network solution for the Canadian travel, tourism, and hospitality industries.
- Yours in Travel Personnel Agency, Inc.: yoursintravel.com

    Yours in Travel Personnel Agency, Inc. is the nation's largest recruitment source for the travel, tourism, transportation, and hospitality industries; it services four continents.

About the Authors

ROBERT SCOTT MILNE has been a full-time freelance travel writer since 1972. Before that he was an encyclopedia editor for sixteen years, first at Collier's Encyclopedia and then at Encyclopedia Americana. He was also moonlighting during those years, writing travel articles for various publications. He became an active member of the Society of American Travel Writers in 1966. The society's Freelance Council gave him a special award for the monthly newsletter he edited and published, *Travelwriter Marketletter*, which gives valuable marketing leads to travel writers and photographers and information on trips offered to them.

Among the periodicals that have published his travel articles are the *New York Times*, *New York Post*, *New York News*, *Chicago Tribune*, and numerous others. Magazines that have featured his work include *Modern Bride*, *Atlantic Monthly*, *Seventeen*, *Cruise Travel*, *Popular Mechanics*, *Travel Holiday*, *Travel Agent Magazine*, *Writer's Digest*, and more. He has also written for Exxon, Texaco, and other travel guides. He has written thousands of articles for the two encyclopedias previously mentioned and for many other encyclopedias and yearbooks. Among the books to which he has contributed are *The Complete Guide to Writing Nonfiction*, *Around the World with the Experts*, *The Great Escape*, and *Mrs. Siu's Chinese Cookbook*.

From 1972 through 1989 he maintained his own office—the envy of the travel-writing world—in the Plaza Hotel in New York City, then moved to the Waldorf-Astoria. Today, with his Vienna-born wife, Gaby, who is a musician, he lives in Elmsford, New York.

MARGUERITE "MIMI" BACKHAUSEN is the current editor and publisher of *Travelwriter Marketletter*. She met Robert S. Milne in 1987 and assisted him part-time with research, computerizing his operations, and putting *Travelwriter Marketletter* on the Internet. Her full-time job was in sales for a large software company, where she was responsible for the travel industry in southern Florida. Love and her passion for new adventures led her to Düsseldorf, Germany, where she currently resides with her German husband, Herbert.